Children Teach Children

ALAN GARTNER

MARY CONWAY KOHLER

FRANK RIESSMAN

Children Teach Children
Learning by Teaching

HARPER & ROW, PUBLISHERS

New York : Evanston : San Francisco : London

1817

FOR OUR CHILDREN

Jonathan, Rachel, Daniel

John, Cathy, Richard

Robin, Janet, Jeffrey

STANDARD BOOK NUMBER: 06-013553-0

LIBRARY OF CONGRESS CATALOG CARD NUMBER: 75-83619

Contents

PHOTOGRAPHS FOLLOW PAGE 52

Acknowledgments

No book is the product of the authors alone. And we are especially indebted to a large number of people who have not only helped us but who have contributed to the development of learning through teaching programs throughout the country. First, we want to acknowledge our debt to the tens of thousands of young people who have participated in these programs, who have shown through their strength and commitment the power of learning through teaching. Specifically, we want to thank those who have developed teaching and training materials, some of which are contained in this book. Also, we want to thank those who have administered these programs and for having taken the time and effort from the heavy responsibilities of program operation to have written reports and studies which we were able to draw upon; we have sought to acknowledge their individual work in the text.

All who work in this field owe a special debt to Peggy and Ronald Lippitt and to Herbert Thelen who have done much to pave the way and who continue to make important contributions. We want to thank them for their kindness and assistance. Gerald Weinstein has been instrumental in the conception and design of the Youth Tutoring Youth program and its success is in no small part a reflection of the quality of his contribution.

Colleagues of each of us have made special contributions—Harriet Johnson in digging out many of the reports and studies; Lorraine Kavanagh for her astute comments; and Leonard P. R. Granick for his advice concerning evaluation. Joseph Gurney was kind enough to allow close observation and participation in the "Each One Teach One" program at his school in Yonkers, New York, and Ralph Melaragno and Gerald Newmark were both cordial hosts and prompt question answerers concerning their program at Pocoima, California.

Audrey Gartner kindly prepared the index. Marilyn Boyce, Dorothy Grant, Bonnie Prives, and Thelma Reid were careful typists and critics of what seemed to be all too many drafts, with their multitude of insertions and corrections.

Alan Gartner is Associate Director, New Careers Development Center, New York University, and author of *Paraprofessionals and Their Performance*. He was formerly Executive Director, Economic Opportunity Council of Suffolk, and before that Community Relations Director, CORE.

Mary Conway Kohler is Executive Director, National Commission on Resources for Youth. She was Chairman of the panel on "The Rights of Children" at the 1970 White House Conference on Children. She was formerly Director of the Neighborhood Youth Corps in New York City, a member of the New York City Board of Education, and Referee of the Juvenile Court in San Francisco, California.

Frank Riessman is Professor of Educational Sociology, New York University, and editor of *Social Policy*. He is the author of several books, including *The Culturally Deprived Child*, and co-author with Arthur Pearl of *New Careers for the Poor*.

Foreword

Children and youth learn far more when performing the teaching role than when acting as students in the classroom. This principle has been known for centuries, but the development of practices that embody it within the structure of the school systems of today is a very recent achievement. This volume reports the experiences of current projects in which young people learn through teaching and outlines the conditions under which successful programs are carried on.

Adolescents have a difficult time in a modern industrial society. As they approach adulthood, they want successful experience in responsible positions in which their activities are appreciated and the results of their work are significant. They seek reassurance that they are needed and that they are becoming effective adults. Instead, most of the current institutions of work and of social and civic action have no significant, recognized places for children and youth. Young people are kept out of adult life in the insulated and isolated islands of school and college. Responsible teaching tasks can furnish important adult roles for many youths, and can meet these needs in whole or in part.

Group instruction is inadequate to stimulate and guide the learning of children whose backgrounds, interests, habits, or practices are markedly different from the typical ones for whom the instructional program was designed. This has become critical today when the virtual elimination of unskilled labor and the complexity of political, social and economic problems faced by our citizens make it imperative for everyone to learn and to continue learning throughout life. We now know that somewhere between 15 and 25 percent of American children do not attain the education required for employment other than unskilled nor the competence required for responsible citizenship. These so-called disadvantaged children require learning programs where each one can begin with tasks appropriate for his background and proceed sequentially to more and more advanced learning, mastering each step as he moves along. This means much more individualization of instruction than is possible in the classrooms as they are now organized. This presents opportunities for service by adolescent youth that can enable them to make significant progress toward adulthood. Properly designed, there can be developed a mutually rewarding relationship between the child requiring individual attention to stimulate and guide his learning and the young person needing to undertake responsible work of recognized importance. This is the great significance of the programs described in this book.

Although there are other kinds of projects that can be worked out to meet this need, youth teaching programs have some particularly favorable characteristics. In the first place, the direct relationship between the child and the youth makes it easy for the child to recognize that someone cares about his learning and tries to help him, and the youth can readily see that he is needed and that his successful efforts are appreciated. Heretofore, young people have been heavily dependent upon parents and teachers to approve or disapprove their activities. Now, they can obtain direct reinforcement from the persons being served. This is seen by youth as being more "real," less biased, less a means of "manipulating them."

In the second place, for most adolescents, the demands of a well-selected teaching task are neither too difficult nor too easy. They have had years of experience as students, and through this they have obtained a fairly detailed concept of teaching and learning. They are not thrown into a completely novel environment. However, they can be given considerable freedom to plan their teaching strategies, to develop materials and to adapt their plans and procedures to the situations they encounter with the individual child. It is not a routine task, as most chores are. There are wide limits for exploration and invention. They quickly recognize that they must learn to observe, to read, to plan, and to appraise their own efforts. Yet, almost without exception they experience success. Almost all children respond to the attention given them and the efforts made in their behalf.

In the third place, most youth find the teaching situation one in which they can explore real career possibilities. This is rarely true of chores or of other common jobs for young people because most such tasks lead to dead ends. To encourage this exploration, the U.S. Office of Education is recognizing and supporting programs of teacher preparation and development which recruit high school students, support them in youth teaching projects and furnish opportunities for career ladders in the field of education based on their high school experience. This support has special significance for those with limited financial means.

The National Commission on Resources for Youth, of which Mary Conway Kohler is the Executive Director, has taken the leadership in developing and expanding youth teaching projects throughout the nation. Currently 250 school systems are furnishing opportunities for some of their young people to help children encountering learning difficulties. Both children and youth are improving their educational progress, and both are finding mutually satisfactory relationships. This report of experiences and the analysis of the processes involved will make an important contribution to educational thought and action.

Ralph W. Tyler
Chicago, Illinois
March 10, 1971

CHAPTER I

Introduction: Every Child a Teacher

From ancient Rome to present-day California, from the Soviet Union to Great Britain to Cuba, there is mounting evidence that a very simple principle may provide a basic strategy for a leap in the learning of children.

It has long been obvious that children learn from their peers, but a more significant observation is that *children learn more from teaching other children.* From this a major educational strategy follows: namely, that every child must be given the opportunity to play the teaching role, because it is through playing this role that he may really learn how to learn.

Mobilization for Youth, a New York City antipoverty program, states that over a five-month period in which older children tutored younger children with reading difficulties, those tutored gained 6.0 months while the tutors gained an extraordinary 3.4 *years. A leap of this magnitude is the order of achievement that must be striven for in the schools of America.*

The experience of the 1960s seems to indicate that the key to learning is individualization, and the use of the student or pupil as a teacher is one way to increase this individualization. The concept of learning through teaching appears to be one of those basic ideas which do work, and it is finding a place in an enormous variety of settings, from the Youth Tutoring Youth programs of the National Commission on Resources for Youth and the cross-age learning experiments of the Lippitts to the Pocoima project in California, where the entire school is directed toward becoming a "tutorial community."

Cross-culturally, various learning through teaching derivatives are to be found, in Cuba, where the Each One Teach One approach is being applied; in Britain, in the infant schools; in the Soviet Union, where one class of pupils adopts another class; and in America, in a variety of programs—for example, Myron Woolman's Vineland program—that do not have as their central emphasis learning through teaching.

RECENT HISTORY—LEARNING THROUGH TEACH-
ING IN THE SIXTIES

Children have been teaching other children throughout history, in manifold settings. The method occurred in one-room schoolhouses, it was central in the Lancaster system, and it is an important ingredient in the Montessori approach, in which the older, more advanced children are utilized to teach the younger, less advanced ones.

In most of these programs, and in the early tutoring programs in the United States, the general emphasis was on improving the learning of the recipient—the tutee. The general finding was that while the recipient may improve a small amount in his learning, there are no qualitative leaps, break-throughs, or improvements of great magnitude on the cognitive indices utilized.

It was in the early 1960s, however, that more strongly directed attention was focused on the potentially significant benefits that may accrue to the tutor.

Peggy and Ronald Lippitt, working in Detroit, Michigan, set up cross-age learning situations whereby fourth-grade pupils with reading problems were assigned to the tutelage of sixth-grade pupils who were also experiencing reading difficulties. The Lippitts found that while the fourth-graders made significant progress, the sixth-graders also learned from the experience, and thus the Lippitts also came to see that Learning Through Teaching was an important principle of learning —although they did not emphasize that the child teacher was the chief beneficiary.

Working at Mobilization for Youth in the early sixties, Frank Riessman observed the rather extensive tutoring program that had been established in which high school youngsters were trained to tutor disadvantaged elementary school youngsters who were doing poorly in school. It seemed from impressionistic observations that while the tutees enjoyed the tutoring sessions, there was no great improvement in their learning. What increasingly stood out, on the other hand, was the fact that the tutors really appeared to be "turned on" by what they were doing. They were not only excited about it, and deriving a new, heightened self-esteem from it, but they also seemed much more interested in the whole learning process. It looked as though they were acquiring a new attitude toward learning, new skills, and, perhaps even more important, new awareness about learning and studying. In a sense they were beginning to *learn how to learn* and to manage their own learning. They were acquiring new learning "sets," and there were some indications that these new sets, skills, and attitudes were beginning to be transferred out to the many different learning experiences in which they were involved. Thus, a tutor who was teaching arithmetic to an elementary school youngster appeared to show self-improvement in many different subjects other than mathematics, although including mathematics. More than that, in many cases the tutors seemed to acquire a new self-conscious, analytic orientation in dealing with all kinds of problems, not just academic work.

These impressionistic observations led MFY's research staff, in particular Robert Cloward and his associates, to develop carefully controlled studies to assess what was occurring. They found striking gains in the achievement scores of the tutors, gains that far exceeded those of the tutees. Unfortunately, most of the cognitive measures that have been employed, not only at MFY but elsewhere, have thus far been largely restricted to achievement tests. There is a great need to develop new, expanded indices related to learning sets, creativity, learning how to learn, analytic thinking, curiosity, and the like. Such measures would help to codify, or perhaps disprove, the earlier impressionistic observations at MFY and the later reports emanating from many LTT projects.

Commenting upon both the MFY and Lippitt experiences, Riessman observed that children "operating in a teaching context . . . may profit . . . from the cognitive mechanisms associated with learning through teaching. They [the tutors] need to learn the material better in order to teach it. Finally, the status and prestige dimensions attached to the teacher role may accrue unforeseen benefits."[1]

Since these beginnings in the early sixties, there has been an enormously rapid spread of various types of tutorial pro-

1. Frank Riessman, "The 'Helper-Therapy' Principle," *Social Work,* 10, no. 2 (April 1965): 30.

grams increasingly emphasizing the importance of the teaching role. In 1968 Herbert Thelen listed some two dozen programs. The National Commission on Resources for Youth's "Youth Tutoring Youth" programs, developed by Mary Conway Kohler, are in operation in over 250 school systems (see Chapter IV). The Career Opportunities Program, operating in 131 communities, incorporates a National Commission-designed "Youth Tutoring Youth" component. As previously mentioned, an entire school in Pocoima, California, is focused around learning through teaching. The bibliography of this book includes additional programs, and there are surely many more.

EDUCATIONAL TRENDS AND LTT

It is not surprising that great interest in learning through teaching should arise at the present time. The LTT concept is related to a number of highly significant current trends: decentralizing of teaching, differentiated staffing, the individualization of instruction, the self-help and the human potential movements, the need for more teaching resources, the growing criticism of competitiveness in the schools and the demand for more cooperative learning situations, the use of the consumer of the service as a service giver, the demand for accountability in the schools and the recognition of the schools' waste and inefficiency, and the great new emphasis on participatory processes. There is, as well, the antipoverty focus, with its recognition that large numbers of disadvantaged youngsters have not been contacted by the usual curriculum and forms of teaching (it is interesting to observe that Learning Through Teaching and most of the tutorial programs have begun in poverty areas), the recognition that the teacher is not the sole repository of knowledge and the concomitant

5

demystification of the learning process, the increased interest in the Montessori methods, and the popularity of such informal learning as TV's *Sesame Street*.

There is increasing recognition today that learning need not be a win-lose game in which some pupils presumably learn a good deal in a competitive grading system and others do not. There is a need for what William Glasser calls *Schools Without Failure*. In the LTT design it is possible for all children to learn effectively through the process of teaching other children, and learning can therefore become much more of a non-zero-sum game.

Herbert Thelen observes:

> The idea of students learning through helping each other is a very promising alternative to the traditional system of learning through competing with each other. It also makes the acquisition of knowledge and skills valuable, not in the service of competition for grades but as the means for personally significant interaction with others.[2]

It is possible, then, to move from the present nonindividualized and competitive system to an individualized and cooperative one.

Donald Durrell at Boston University has commented that a great deal of time in the classroom is wasted when the teacher asks a student a question and the whole class sits passively by while the pupil responds in this one-to-one dialogue. Durrell proposes many ways whereby large numbers of youngsters can be active simultaneously, and, of course, learning through teaching allows for much more simultaneous involvement of all the youngsters. More, it constrains toward much more pervasive active participation; educational psychology has long observed that the active learner is the better learner. Of

2. Herbert A. Thelen, "The Humane Person Defined" (Paper presented at the Secondary Education Leadership Conference, St. Louis, Missouri, November 1967).

course, if the active learner learns how to learn, all the better, and if he acquires significant learning attitudes, still better— then the transfer to other subjects and areas will be greater.

Dwight Allen, Dean, School of Education, University of Massachusetts, has led the way in proposing differentiated staffing in schools. Much of his emphasis has been upon differentiated roles for teachers, but included also are all types of auxiliary paraprofessional personnel, and there is no reason why tutors functioning in the teaching role should not be included as well. This allows the teacher to play some very different kinds of roles; in Klopf's and Bowman's formulation it permits the teacher to orchestrate or manage the learning process more, to be a resource person—as in the British infant schools—to utilize highly specific advanced techniques for particular purposes, and to play a much more specialized role.

The Lippitts and Herbert Thelen have been very much concerned about the emotional or affective benefits that surround and contextualize LTT. The Lippitts observed that it is rare for older youngsters to have the opportunity to play a constructive, socializing, positive role with younger children, but that the cross-age model allows for and encourages this greatly. Thelen notes that LTT may play an important role in combating prejudice. He states that ". . . student tutoring built into the regular classroom learning process capitalizes on heterogeneity and therefore is a method through which racial class and integration can be achieved. It is specially intriguing to think of the possibilities of Negroes helping whites, of younger children helping older ones, of ethnic minority members helping the majority."[3]

3. Ibid.

INDIVIDUALIZATION

One of the major observations in the current period is that the key to learning is individualization—the patterning of learning to suit the individual, his idiom, his style, his way of learning. In essence, an ultimate objective might be for every child to have his own teacher, and perhaps one way of achieving this is to have each pupil play the teacher role. As a tutor, he learns through teaching, and he also learns as a recipient, as a tutee when he is being taught. Of course, another way of achieving this individualization is through various computer-aided forms of programmed instruction, and to some extent, of course, these two approaches can be combined when the tutor uses and monitors programmed materials for the tutee, as in Woolman's model. But in fairness it must be said that learning through teaching essentially is an emphasis on *learning from people*. It is a people-oriented approach to learning in contrast to the more machine-oriented approaches. Another contrast is also important here: most programmed learning is, by necessity, highly sequenced, ordered, and preplanned. The learning through teaching model can be much more informal, idiosyncratic, and open ended, following the needs and interests of the learner at the moment, although, of course, it is possible for the LTT design to be highly formalized and sequenced. The crucial point, however, is that it is individualized; it can be attuned to the style and way of learning of the individual child as well as to the individual child acting as a teacher. A teacher for every child is by no means impossible. The new motto may very well be that everybody is teaching and, of course, everybody is learning.

LTT AND THE HELPER THERAPY PRINCIPLE

Some of the same principles that are operative in LTT may function in a wide variety of other settings, especially in the rapidly expanding self-help movement. Riessman noted in formulating the "helper therapy principle" that:

> People with a problem helping other people who have the same problem in more severe form (e.g., Alcoholics Anonymous), is a simple age old approach, well known to all group therapists. But in using this approach—and there is a marked current increase in its use—we may be placing the emphasis on the wrong person in centering attention on the individual receiving the help. More attention might well be given . . . to the person who is providing the assistance—*the helper—because it is he who really improves!*
> While it may be uncertain that people *receiving* help are always benefited, it seems much clearer that the people *giving* the help are profiting from their role. This appears to be the case in a wide variety of group "therapies," including Synanon (for drug addicts), Recovery Incorporated (for psychologically disturbed people), Alcoholics Anonymous (for alcoholics), SCORE (Charles Slack's program for delinquents).
> Perhaps then our strategy ought to be to *devise ways of creating* more *helpers.* Or to be more exact: how to transform receivers of help into dispensers of help; how to reverse their roles, how to structure the situation so that receivers of help will be placed in roles requiring the giving of assistance.[4]

Of course, the "helper-therapy principle" has been seen in contexts where the helper is in some way deficient and gains from the helping. This is not necessarily the case in learning through teaching, which can benefit all children; rather, the commonality with programs such as those discussed here is

4. Riessman, "The 'Helper-Therapy' Principle," pp. 27 f.

the power of the helping mechanism in its effect upon the person playing the helper role.

WHY DOES LTT WORK?

As we shall see, there are a great many different reasons both at the emotional and cognitive levels why learning through teaching is effective. It is because it is effective at so many different levels and through so many different mechanisms that the principle acquires its enormous power and potential.

Because helping other children to learn or playing the helper role is exciting and novel, it may provide an excellent contact to learning. As Weinstein and Fantini indicate, the contact stage is a first crucial stage in the learning process. For a child to be interested in the curriculum, he must be contacted, he must be connected to the material. Learning through teaching may provide an avenue to this contact.

But perhaps even more important, the principle may assist the child tutor to *learn how to learn*, which is a much deeper dimension of the learning process and one that may carry far more multiplier effects.

If one learns how to learn, one can be a learner in a great number of areas. A child, in order to teach another child material, needs to learn the material better in the first place; he needs to organize it, needs to observe another learner, and make contact with that learner. In essence, he must become a manager of learning and he may become more aware about learning; all this contributes to learning how to learn.

In a sense, learning through teaching is an illustration of role theory; an individual playing a new role, whether it be the teacher role or the helper role in a therapeutic context, develops new behavior patterns related to that role, acquires new experiences, new feelings, new consciousness. It may unleash new energies in the child, build his self-concept—"I must be fairly good if I can help somebody else"—and the competency acquired from giving this help furthers the development and self-confidence.

As we shall see in Chapter III, there are a great variety of cognitive and affective mechanisms that support and help explain learning through teaching, but learning how to learn and developing self-esteem through playing the teacher role are perhaps central.

SYSTEM CHANGE OR ATROPHY THROUGH BUREAUCRACY

One of the special purposes of this book is to draw attention to the unique power of the learning through teaching principle and the numerous mechanisms that may account for its effectiveness. In a sense, we are suggesting that the principle needs to be utilized much more consciously, energetically, and in a focused fashion in order to produce learning and developmental growth of sharp magnitude with wide transfer. We want to see improvements that go far beyond, although including, achievement tests and school grades. A carefully managed conscious exploitation of the learning through teaching principle should produce a great multiplicity of benefits, such as positive attitudes toward learning (being "turned on" by learning), learning how to learn and how to organize one's learning, improved use of the tools of learning, a variety of learning skills, and expanded self-esteem. To produce these kinds of results, so that learning through teaching can operate at its fullest, we will have to develop educational strategies whereby every child is assisted in playing the tutor role. This is no simple assignment. It will require great managerial innovation and administrative skill because many programs that function on a small-scale demonstration basis fail to live up to their promise when instituted on a large-scale, system-wide basis. Chapter V will give special attention to these issues.

Unfortunately, we have all too often witnessed sound innovative programs that exhibit beneficial, significant results on the small scale but fail when implemented within a larger school system. Projects such as Higher Horizons in New York City, Deutsch's work with preschool children, and many others that seem to work on a small scale have not been able to withstand and combat the negative forces of bureaucratization that seem to accompany institutionalization in large school systems. Where the learning through teaching concept has been expanded to an entire school (Yonkers, New York, Pocoima, California), the programs are facing powerful obstacles.

A significant portion of this book, therefore, will be directed toward problems related to administrative management, or, to put it simply, "How To Do It in Your School"—how to prevent the diluting of the program as it moves from the experimental, innovative, demonstration phase to a larger institutional phase; how to prevent its negative bureaucratization; how to develop a school culture that supports it and management procedures that implement it fully; how to train a cadre to carry out the program flexibly; how to free the teachers of their preconceived notions, which fence in the creativity and spontaneity of children; how to prevent all the various interferences and distractions so characteristic of traditional school culture; how to capture and use some of the features that characterize the innovative demonstration; and how to make the transition from the demonstration phase to the larger phase in stages.

Finally, attention must be paid to problems of evaluation. A major finding of one of the most important studies, the

CHILDREN TEACH CHILDREN

LEARNING BY TEACHING

Alan Gartner   Mary Kohler   Frank Riessman

Cloward study of the MFY program, indicates that while the reading achievement of the tutors improves, their school grades do not. Why is this so? Should we try to overcome it? How can we measure the great variety of cognitive and affective changes that take place? What new types of measures are needed, measures of learning how to learn, curiosity, feeling of competency?

———has not quite turned against school, but I'm
afraid he soon will. He feels teachers are unfair
and no one listens to him and feels that he is getting
too far behind to catch up. I spent considerable
time listening to him let off steam. He is a
good person, and we shouldn't lose him![1]

A Survey of Learning Through Teaching Programs

The fact of people teaching and learning from each other has existed and is documented down through the ages. "As early as the 1st century, the great Roman teacher, Quintilian, pointed out in his *Institutio Oratoria* how much the younger children can learn from the older children in the same class. In Hindu schools the use of mutual instruction dates back to ancient times."[2] In *Didactica Magna*, probably completed in 1632 but published first in 1849, the Moravian teacher, John Comenius, wrote:

The saying, "He who teaches others, teaches himself," is very

1. Comment by a tutor in the San Diego, California, Youth Tutoring Youth program.
2. Benjamin Wright, "Should Children Teach?" *Elementary School Journal* 60, no. 7 (April 1960): 353.

true, not only because constant repetition impresses a fact indelibly on the mind, but because the process of teaching in itself gives a deeper insight into the subject taught. . . . The gifted Joachim Fortius used to say that . . . if a student wished to make progress, he should arrange to give lessons daily in the subjects which he was studying, even if he had to hire his pupils.[3]

However, it was requirements of the Industrial Revolution in the late eighteenth century that aroused public interest in education, and the advantages of mutual instruction were recognized and discussed. Today the most widely known exponent of what came to be called the monitorial system is Joseph Lancaster, an English Quaker. Because he did not have the money to hire teachers to help him run the school he opened in 1798 for poor children, Lancaster was forced to utilize the children themselves as teachers. His book, *Improvements in Education* (1806), documents the positive results achieved through this "spontaneous" experiment. Through his untiring proselytizing and propagandizing, models based on the original school and its theories were immensely popular for at least thirty years in the United States, to which he emigrated in 1818.

Similar ideas were developed by Andrew Bell, a rival of Lancaster, at the same period. Bell summarized his beliefs, stating:

That the teacher profits far more by teaching than the scholar does by learning, is a maxim of antiquity, which all experience confirms—"*Docemur docendo*"—"He who teaches learns."[4]

The ideas of Lancaster and Bell and their schools eventually fell into disrepute. Utilizing the students themselves as teachers

---

3. John Amos Comenius, *The Great Didactic*, Part II, trans. M. W. Keatinge (London: A. and C. Black, Ltd., 1921), p. 47.
4. Andrew Bell, *Bell's Mutual Tuition and Moral Discipline* (London: C. J. G. & F. Livingston, 1832), p. 75.

was extremely economical, and once the focus shifted from the positive, cognitive effects of the monitorial-tutorial system to the economic advantages, the implementation of this powerful idea became mechanized, quality was replaced by quantity, and evaluation was unimportant. There was eventually a public outcry, and as a greater supply of professional teachers became available, the monitorial system was no longer necessary.

William Bentley Fowle, a nineteenth-century educator and mutual instruction advocate, would not allow the Lancaster disaster to deter him from its use. He justified his abhorrence of traditional school structure in the following way:

> The best disciplined minds are often found in those children who, by what the world terms a misfortune, are thrown upon their own resources, and early accustomed to the exercise of their moral and intellectual faculties. . . . Do I err when I say that no good opportunity for such exercise is afforded in common schools, where each is required to hoard his knowledge, and is forbidden to impart it to others, where intercourse is prohibited, and whispering is high treason, where change of place, if not of position, is punished as depravity, where implicit obedience is the divine right of the teacher, and the divine wrong of the pupil; where, in fact, the best pupil is he who most nearly resembles an automaton?[5]

Fowle goes on to specify why students' teaching is a preferable technique:

> By teaching the younger children, the more advanced are constantly reviewing their studies, not by learning merely, but by the surer method of teaching what they have learned to others.[6]

5. William Bentley Fowle, *The Teachers' Institute* (New York: A. S. Barnes, 1866).
6. Ibid.

Fowle perceived other advantages of the mutual instruction system, cognitive as well as social and political:

> One hour, (the child) may govern his class according to fixed laws enacted by the master, and well understood by every pupil; the very next hour, he may be subject to one of the very pupils that he had just directed. The monitorial plan, as I used it, is the true democratic one: the children all had a chance at the offices, though only the qualified and the deserving were appointed. Being sometimes governed, children are less likely to become imperious; and sometimes commanding, they will not too easily become servile.[7]

And he suggested a learner-focused teaching style:

> The art of teaching depends more upon adapting the explanation to the capacity of the learner than upon the amount of knowledge accumulated by the teacher. Is it unreasonable then to suppose that the explanations of children may sometimes be better suited to the understanding of children than those of adults would be? I am not ashamed to own that I often called on my monitors to explain what I had failed to make a little scholar apprehend.[8]

Thus we can see that motives of benefit to both tutor and tutee were incorporated in earlier versions of children teaching one another.

CROSS-AGE LEARNING

In the early 1960s Peggy and Ronald Lippitt (and associates) began work using older elementary and junior high school students to work with younger elementary grade children. Similar projects were beginning at New York City's

7. Ibid.
8. Ibid.

Mobilization for Youth[9] and in the homework-assisting projects later established in that city's public schools. The work of the Lippitts focused upon the process of socialization among the older children[10] and assistance to the younger children.[11] The initial projects were at the University of Michigan Laboratory School, at a neighborhood public school, and at a summer day camp.[12]

The Lippitts' first project involved twenty-seven sixth-graders assisting in a kindergarten. A pair of the older children helped out, three days a week, for forty-five minutes. Twice weekly the older children met to discuss the experience of working with the younger ones, and to improve the work done with them. The next year, 1962, the initial effort having been successful within its limited scope, the program was expanded to two Detroit public schools, with sixth-graders helping in the first through fourth grades.

> They helped individuals in the younger classrooms with the skills of reading, writing, arithmetic and spelling. They were also used as assistants in physical education, and laboratory assistants in Social Studies. . . . Each academic helper had a helping relationship to one young pupil.[13]

In addition to the two school projects, a cross-age program

9. Robert Cloward, "Studies in Tutoring," *The Journal of Experimental Education* 36, no. 1 (Fall 1967): 14–25.
10. Peggy Lippitt and John E. Lohman, "Cross-Age Relationships—An Educational Resource," *Children* 12, no. 3 (May–June 1965): 113–117.
11. R. S. Fox, R. Lippitt, and J. E. Lohman, "Teaching of Social Science Material in the Elementary School" (Final report, Cooperative Research Project, E-011, U.S. Office of Education, n.d.), Chapter V.
12. Lippitt and Lohman, "Cross-Age Relationships . . ."; Fox, Lippitt, and Lohman, "Teaching of Social Science Material . . ."; Peggy Lippitt, Jeffrey Eiseman, and Ronald Lippitt, *Cross-Age Helping Program: Orientation, Training, and Related Materials* (Ann Arbor: University of Michigan, Center for Research on Utilization of Scientific Knowledge, Institute for Social Research, 1969), pp. 19 ff.
13. Fox, Lippitt, and Lohman, "Teaching of Social Science Material . . . ," p. 68.

was initiated at a day camp for children, ages four through twelve, of staff members at the National Training Laboratories, Bethel, Maine.[14] Three specific strategies were used to facilitate the cross-age relationship. First, four times a day activities were structured to enable the children to interact with each other—at crafts, at town meetings, at lunch, and at swimming. Second, specific training was given to the older children in cross-age relationships. And third, camp staff were trained, a week before the camp opened and at meetings at the beginning and end of each camp day.

Underlying these efforts were five assumptions:

much of the process of socialization involves use by younger children of the behavior and attitudes of older children as models for their own behavior. This process has great potentiality for planned development as an effective educational force, provided that children are trained appropriately for their role as socialization agents;

involvement of older children in a collaborative program with adults to help younger children will have a significant socialization impact on the older children because of (1) the important motivational value of a trust- and responsibility-taking relationship with adults around a significant task, and (2) the opportunity to work through—with awareness but at a safe emotional distance—some of their own problems of relationships with their siblings and peers;

assisting in a teaching function will help the "teaching students" to test and develop their own knowledge, and also help them discover the significance of that knowledge;

both younger learners and their adult teachers will be significantly helped in "academic" learning activities through the utilization of older children;

a child will develop a more realistic sense of his own ability and present state of development . . . if he has an opportunity

14. Ibid., pp. 82–93.

to help children younger than himself to acquire skills which he already possesses and to develop positive relationships with children older than himself.[15]

Anecdotal reports indicated that both the younger and older children were helped. For the younger ones there was improved performance, interest, attentiveness, motivation, and opportunity for individual recognition.[16] The older children, too, gained in terms of their attitudes, interest in school, and ability to work cooperatively with other children. A teacher of an older group related:

> The children return from helping sessions with an increased will to do well in their own work. This made the time spent on the work in class more effective. It increased the self-respect and belief in their own ability of my defeated children, thereby contributing much to making them capable of learning.[17]

From their experience with these initial projects, five types of children were identified as those who benefit especially from cross-age experience:

> Those who for some reason find it difficult to be successful with their own age groups.

> Children who are the youngest in their families and who never had a chance to develop the skills of being "an older helper."

> The oldest in a family who has never had a "bigger" boy or girl to look up to or to model after.

> Siblings who have not had a chance before to be in the same educational environment as "equals."

> A younger child who has never had a chance for close ob-

15. Lippitt and Lohman, "Cross-Age Relationships . . . ," passim.
16. Fox, Lippitt, and Lohman, "Teaching of Social Science Material . . . ," passim; Lippitt and Lohman, "Cross-Age Relationships . . . ," passim.
17. Fox, Lippitt, and Lohman, "Teaching of Social Science Material . . . ," p. 79.

servation or companionship of an older child of the same sex who can be an inspiration for taking the next step in "grown-upness."[18]

A more elaborate program was established in a Detroit public school complex—a high school, a junior high school, and an elementary school. Sixty-eight children participated. The older pupils met with the younger ones for a half hour a day three or four times a week. They helped in activities ranging from drills on spelling words, mathematics tables, and Latin vocabulary to making bookcases, sewing, and publishing a class paper. Teachers of the younger children reported academic gains for practically all of the children involved, greater class participation, greater effort, extra work being done, better attendance, greater attentiveness, less fooling around, greater ability to express oneself, increased willingness to accept help, and greater self-confidence, self-respect, and self-image.[19]

The high school tutors, given a list of categories, were asked to check off whether or not their own attitudes toward schools, teachers, and the future had changed.

> Seventeen out of the twenty-four (71%) felt they had changed their attitudes toward at least one of these references, eight changed in their attitudes toward two or more. Of these seventeen who experienced a change in attitude, only one changed in a negative direction.[20]

When asked to check other changes in themselves that they felt resulted from the cross-age tutoring program, the children gave the following responses:[21]

18. Ibid., pp. 93–96.
19. Lippitt, Eiseman, and Lippitt, *Cross-Age Helping Program . . .*, pp. 2–6.
20. Ibid., p. 20.
21. Ibid., pp. 7 f.

NO. CHECKING	CHANGE IN SELF
19	Understanding others better
10	Being more considerate of others
19	Being more patient
6	Getting along with others
15	Feeling more useful
18	Greater self-confidence

It appears from the data that positive changes resulted for both tutors and tutees.

While the pioneering work of the Lippitts and their colleagues includes concern for the cognitive area, their special interest in socialization strategies led to a lesser focus in the cognitive area, and perhaps concomitantly, an absence of "hard" evaluative data. At the same time as the Lippitts began their work in the Detroit public schools, Mobilization for Youth, New York City, one of the initial projects established by the antidelinquency efforts of the Kennedy administration, undertook a program in which older children tutored younger ones in an after-school effort and Mobilization's program gave greater attention to the cognitive area.

THE MFY HOMEWORK HELPER PROGRAM

Under the direction of a Mobilization for Youth program coordinator, in February 1963 nine tutorial centers were set up in neighborhood elementary schools, a Board of Education licensed teacher in charge within each school. The licensed teacher was responsible for weekly in-service meetings and all other activities related to the tutoring in the center. A careful evaluation of the MFY program was conducted for the period from November 1963 to June 1964. Experimental and control group tutees were randomly divided into groups according to predetermined comparable samples. There were 410 experimental pupils and 185 control pupils; about half of both groups were Puerto Rican and 30 percent were Negro. Experimental pupils were tutored either two or four hours per week and control pupils did not participate in tutoring at all. Improving reading achievement was the major goal of the program, and students were pre- and post-tested.

> At the beginning of the program, the average fourth-grade subject was reading at grade 3.5, eight months below grade level, and the average fifth-grade pupil was reading at grade 4.2, one year and one month below grade level. There were no significant differences between experimental and control subjects.[22]

The following describes the results for the *tutees* on the post-test:

> In terms of grade equivalents, the four-hour pupils showed an average of six months' reading improvement in five months' time whereas the control pupils showed only three and a half months' growth during the same period. The growth rate of the controls—or, more accurately, their progressive retardation —approximates the average rate for Puerto Rican elementary school children in the Mobilization area. Thus, the four-hour group not only arrested their retardation but began to catch up. The comparable two-hour group made a gain of five months in reading during the same five-month period. Thus, tutorial assistance results in significant reading improvement providing that the assistance is given as often as four hours a week for a period of 25 weeks.[23]

Of the 240 tutors participating in the program, the mean reading level was 10.0. However, 22 percent scored lower

22. Cloward, "Studies in Tutoring," p. 17.
23. Ibid, p. 17.

than 8.0 on the reading achievement test. Fifty-two percent of the tutors were tenth-grade students, and 19 percent were Puerto Rican and 18 percent were Negro. Following seven months of participation in the tutoring sessions, as well as two weeks of training before the tutoring began and weekly in-service sessions during the program with licensed teachers, the *tutors* showed:

> . . . a mean growth of 3.4 years as compared with 1.7 years for the control subjects.
>
> Since an alternate form of the same test was used in the post-study administration, it may be that a substantial portion of the increase for both groups was due to their increased familiarity with the complex directions for taking the test. It should be noted, however, that experimental subjects showed twice as much improvement as the controls (who had also taken the same pre-test at the same time and with the experimental group).[24]

Other conclusions raise some interesting issues. When checking the academic marks of participating tutors immediately before the program with their marks after the program, no significant change was seen to have occurred. Improvement in reading achievement did not seem to affect school grades. Cloward suggests that improvement in school grades may appear at a future time, and not concurrently with the tutoring program. Or perhaps the "Pygmalion" effect was at play here. That is, once a child has been labeled a 70, or C, student by his teacher, the teacher's perception of the child does not alter even when his academic and achievement levels change. Or perhaps the school had so little relationship to real learning and was so boring that there was no opportunity for transfer of learning.

Since 1967 the Homework Helper Program, with support

24. Ibid., p. 22.

from ESEA Title I funds, has operated under the auspices of the New York City Board of Education. In ten New York City school districts there are about 100 centers serving 1,500 tutors and 4,500 tutees. A tutorial assistance center at the Board of Education provides training manuals for staff, including administrators, paraprofessionals, and tutors, and disseminates information. As in the original program, tutors are paid $1.50 to $2.00 per hour.

In 1969 Fordham University's School of Education prepared an evaluation of two of the participating school districts. Data, gathered by the Fordham group through observation, questionnaires, and interviews, showed favorable responses, not unlike the Lippitt group. Tutors believed they helped tutees both in basic skills and in attitudes toward school and study, beliefs that were shared by the tutees. The slim reports of effect upon tutors suggests that they, too, gained. However, there are no hard data, no pre- and post-testing, or no checking of academic grades. The experimental and research design created by Cloward does not seem to have been replicated once the program moved from the demonstration stages to an institutionalized Board of Education program.

THE "CARING RELATIONSHIP"

Herbert Thelen has focused his attention upon the nature of the relationship between tutor and tutee. He has worked with children who are not making it in school and also with emotionally disturbed youngsters. During the spring of 1967 pilot projects were conducted in three Chicago schools, including the University of Chicago's Laboratory School.[25]

25. Herbert A. Thelen, "The Humane Person Defined" (Paper presented at the Secondary Education Leadership Conference, St. Louis, Missouri, November 1967).

Thelen stresses the importance of the groups, and in each school fifteen pupil groups of fifth- or sixth-graders worked with first- or second-graders four to six times a week for thirty to sixty minutes each time. With the younger children activities included teaching games, puppet play, reading, writing a story dictated by the younger child, seeing a movie together and discussing it, demonstrating science experiments, etc. And:

> The older children spent as much time with themselves together as they did with the younger kids. So, we've got two kinds of caring: for each other as they together faced the prospect of the younger children; and each working with the younger child. With each other they prepared themselves to observe and interview the younger ones, discussing their teaching problems; role-playing possible interventions like how to handle the overactive or underactive first grades; practicing their lessons; working on demonstrations or skits; and so on.[26]

Although some of the older children were resistant initially, most soon sought to join; indeed, one went to the length of forging a letter from the principal requesting that she be allowed to participate as a tutor!

For Thelen the tutoring program is not an end itself but an expression of the "caring relationship," one that, he believes, can and should become the central focus of the school. He foresees:

> First, development of more sense of community within the school by cutting across grade lines, and by providing a common interest (teaching) in which students at many different grades can participate.
>
> Second, reduction of cross-cultural, cross-generational, and authority barriers to communication.
>
> Third, changing the climate of the school through its de-

26. Ibid., p. 16. Thelen is working on a five-year NIMH research project, "Use of Small Groups to Adapt Problem Students."

velopment of the norm of concern for each other; substitution of processes of cooperative inquiry for the anxious competitiveness which presently distorts the children's perceptions of each other.

Fourth, enhancing the ego development and self-esteem of the kids. The first success experience of feeling wanted is highly dramatic, and can open the window to a new way of looking at self.

Fifth, letting the students see a new use for subject matter knowledge and thus assimilate it better and even come to want more of it. In the helping relationship, knowledge is the currency of interaction. It is not just to pile up and hand back on a test. Nor is it just to use to make deductions from chemical principles as to whether some reaction will go or not. What we are talking about is *humane* uses of knowledge: for having interaction stimulation, being able to dominate, being able to reach out and make contact with other people through talking about something.

Sixth, giving youngsters a chance to practice the adult role of teacher and visualize the possibility that there may be a place for them in the productive society after all—a great discovery for non-achievement oriented slum kids.

Seventh, offering leadership training to students in the hope that they may become indigenous leaders in their community.

Eighth, increasing by a large factor the amount of teaching going on in school. There could be ten or twenty times as much teaching going on in the school right now, without it costing a cent, if schools would capitalize on some of the student resources they already have.

Ninth is the possibility of individualizing instruction, on a one-to-one tutorial basis.

Tenth, giving the younger kids a big brother or a big sister who can guide them during the year, and it is one of the things I especially want to find out about the helping relationship. Will the older child helping the younger, like the fifth grader helping the first grader, develop a relationship with so much pull, so much value to both sides that it becomes semipermanent? Will they want to find ways to maintain this relationship even outside of the formal activities—in other words, will they move into some kind of a spontaneously developing guidance system on the basis of voluntary choice?

Eleventh, providing remedial resources pinpointed to the kids when they most need help. It is one thing to schedule opportunity for youngsters to get help, but what about having students available who can help in a crisis when the teacher has to keep on with the class?

Twelfth, picking up cues for better teaching and management by watching the more successful "natural teachers" among our own students, especially when they come from backgrounds different from ours.

Thirteenth is a reminder that the helping or adjunct teaching roles might also receive student teachers, parents and helpers from the community.

Finally, one of the things that got us into this in the first place, is the possibility of using tutorial activity as a way to develop the child's own insight into the teaching-learning process so that he can cooperate more effectively with his own teachers in meaningful learning activities. That is, it might contribute to the objective of the child learning how to learn.[27]

YOUTH TUTORING YOUTH

Each of the programs described thus far has been conducted by a school as part of its regular day. The Youth Tutoring Youth program of the National Commission on Resources for Youth differs in that it is an after-school (and/or summer) program run in collaboration with the Neighborhood Youth Corps.[28] Building upon its concern for

27. Ibid., pp. 18 ff.
28. Actually, National Commission on Resources for Youth, Youth Tutoring Youth programs are operated, in some instances, by school systems

meaningful work opportunities for youngsters in the Neighborhood Youth Corps, the National Commission on Resources for Youth proposed to the Corps's sponsor, the U.S. Department of Labor, an experimental program. The design was to employ NYC enrollees who are at least two years behind grade level in reading as tutors to younger underachieving children in ghetto schools. Under subcontract to the Board of Education of Newark, New Jersey, and Philadelphia, Pennsylvania, programs were established in the summer of 1967.[29]

In Philadelphia 120 tutors worked in groups of 20 at six school locations.

In Newark there were 80 tutors at one school. The tutors were both economically and educationally disadvantaged. In both cities tutors were paid $1.25 an hour for 22 hours each week—16 hours spent in tutoring, 6 in training. An additional 6 hours each week was spent in remedial work. Tutoring sessions were usually 2 hours long, 4 days a week.

The program, although having common goals,[30] varied in

alone or as part of programs other than Neighborhood Youth Corps. Here, however, we will confine our discussion to those which are part of the National Commission on Resources for Youth Neighborhood Youth Corps program; Chapter IV will examine the entire NCRY design.

29. National Commission on Resources for Youth, "Youth Tutoring Youth —It Worked" (Report on an In-School Neighborhood Youth Corps Demonstration Project, Manpower Administration, Department of Labor, Contract no. 42-7-001-34, New York City, January 31, 1968).

30. "A number of possibilities were being tested out. These were: —That a school system can operate a tutoring program using underachieving 14- and 15-year olds as tutors. —That indigenous non-professionals can, with training, serve as effective supervisors of such tutors. —That materials appropriate for teaching reading in a tutoring program can be identified and/or developed. —That underachieving and seemingly unmotivated youths of 14 and 15 years can, with proper training, develop the skills and acquire the motivations necessary to teach younger children. —That by providing each tutee with a one-to-one tutoring relationship with an older youth, his reading ability and/or attitude toward learning may be improved. —That tutors, by learning to teach, can learn to learn and will show gains in reading achievement, although no statistically significant gains were expected to emerge over the brief six-week programs. —That by providing each tutor with an opportunity to help a younger child, he can feel the satisfaction of

the two cities. In Newark community involvement was emphasized. A community committee was organized to help recruit tutors and tutees,[31] and to select six community persons to act as tutor supervisors. All were mothers and residents of the area where the program operated. Most had not finished high school; three were leaders of groups who had taken direct action against the Board of Education; all were poor. They received a week of pre-service training in group dynamics and reading instruction. Describing one supervisor, an observer wrote:

> After the tutees had gone, the discussion continued with the tutors—she would look over the reports, ask a question, make a comment—always softly and without being dogmatic, rewording a question if the tutor's response was not adequate or appropriate.[32]

In Philadelphia each of the six centers was directed by an experienced teacher, backed up by six paraprofessional aides. Of the 124 tutors enrolled, 119 stayed all summer. Although the program design called for 4 tutees per tutor, actually 710 tutees enrolled. Each of the centers had a flavor of its own—some using the community as a key learning resource, others using games to learn, still another created a structured school environment. *Central to all was the confidence placed in the tutors as able to teach and learn.*

---

being useful, capable and important, and thus enhance his self-respect, develop a sense of responsibility and participation in the society around him and, hopefully, lessen his estrangement from the school establishment and society. —That the project can successfully demonstrate models for the use of 14- and 15-year olds in a meaningful, educationally-related work assignment which can be readily applicable to a year-round In-School Neighborhood Youth Corps program." [Ibid., pp. 4 f.]

31. There were 80 tutors and before the riot, July 13–17, 1967, 180 tutees. Following the riot, which occurred at the end of the second week of the project, the tutee enrollment dropped to 90. On the first day of the riot all but 2 of the tutors showed up, and on July 18 all were present.

32. NCRY, "Youth Tutoring Youth—It Worked," p. 8.

Tutor achievement in terms of academic growth was measured using the Iowa Silent Reading Tests. At the beginning of the summer the Philadelphia tutors were 0.4 grades behind the expected age level in reading,[33] while in Newark there was 2.9 years' retardation.

In Newark, where the tutors were indeed underachieving youngsters, significant gains were noted in various reading skills, and reading age equivalents leapt 3.7 years. Philadelphia's tutors—who did not really fit the program's criterion of demonstrated reading failure—increased one year in their mean reading age equivalency.[34]

As the NCRY report[35] carefully points out:

No one expects that the Newark tutors really did gain 3.5 years in reading maturity in a mere six weeks. Although some of the gain may have been genuine, there are many explanations—such as test familiarity and pressures for improvement—for the startling rise.[36]

The apparent role of the tutorial staff, especially the six community tutor supervisors, deserves note here. It was their commitment to having the project "prove itself," in the face of perceived antagonism from the Board of Education, that is suggested as a key factor in the "pressures for improvement." Whatever the actual reading gain (and the findings are almost exactly as those reported by Cloward for the MFY program, see above), many other findings are reported.

The care and excitement with which a tutor led a tutee through a challenging lesson, showing that once responsibility is given, it will be accepted—and used for great benefit.

33. The average age of the tutors in Philadelphia was 14.4 years, and 14.5 in Newark.
34. NCRY, "Youth Tutoring Youth—It Worked," p. 20.
35. The evaluation section was prepared by Leonard P. R. Granick.
36. NCRY, "Youth Tutoring Youth—It Worked," p. 20.

The tutors' sustained interest and participation (only 7 of the 200 tutors left the program, and they did so because of illness or a higher paying job).

The increased literacy skills of tutors and tutees, their changed vocational aspirations, and their greater sympathy for the classroom teacher.

The understanding and easy rapport that developed between tutor and tutee, demonstrating that tutors did identify with younger children and found this a way to get at their own problems.

The new pride evident in the tutors as they grew in their new role of "teacher"; and in their own eyes, as well as those of parents, teachers, and tutees.

The books that disappeared from shelves and circulated in the group, as the written work came into their lives in a real way for the first time.

The endless variety of complex and simple materials they devised, as their creativity thrived in attempts to spur tutees.

The new confidence that displayed itself in finding ways to communicate with the tutee in an individual relationship.

The successful participation of sub-professional community people, and the enthusiasm and support they engendered in other parents.[37]

It is these more behavioral goals which are central to the Commission's concerns. "Basically YTY was set up to give tutors a sense of potency . . . to foster a sense of personal effectiveness through a work experience . . . to give meaningful job responsibilities through the task of tutoring."[38]

37. Ibid., pp. 20 f.
38. National Commission on Resources for Youth, "Final report, In-School Neighborhood Youth Corps Project" (Manpower Administration, Department of Labor, Contract no. 42-7-001-34, January 31, 1969), p. 40.

Building upon the successful demonstration in Newark and Philadelphia in the summer of 1967, the National Commission on Resources for Youth has worked to expand YTY programs. The Philadelphia Board of Education introduced an after-school program in the spring of 1968. A conference in May 1968 brought representatives of four city school systems to Philadelphia to observe the program there and introduce other systems to the design. In the summer of 1968 programs were operated in Philadelphia, Detroit, Washington, D.C., and Los Angeles, and in the fall of the same year each of the cities (and San Mateo, California) operated a program. Another conference was held in Washington, D.C., in November 1968, this time with nine districts represented. In January 1969 thirteen school districts operated after-school programs. By the fall of 1970 the number had reached more than 200. And the Office of Education's new Career Opportunities Program, operating in some 131 communities in all 50 states, includes a Youth Tutoring Youth component designed by NCRY.[39]

THE TUTORIAL COMMUNITY

The System Development Corporation, during a research project to develop effective instructional procedures for the teaching of reading-readiness concepts to first-grade Mexican-American students in 1967/68, found that with training and specifically defined behavioral objectives, the tutoring situation involving students as teachers proved most effective. The principal investigators, Newmark and Melaragno, had fifth-

---

39. In the COP program tutoring, in addition to being valuable for tutor and tutee, is seen as being a possible first step on a career ladder in education. See below for a discussion of tutoring as it relates both to learning how to teach and in career decisions leading to becoming a teacher.

and sixth-graders tutor first-graders, as well as first-graders tutor each other.[40]

Newmark and Melaragno concluded that tutoring, to be maximally effective, should be extended to create a "tutorial community," in which everyone is a learner and a teacher. The faculty of Pocoima Elementary School, Los Angeles, voted 38–0 to become part of the Tutorial Project on a school-wide basis. Essential to the program was involvement of the parents and the surrounding community. To accomplish this end, community residents were added to the staff, and en-counter groups between teachers, parents, and staff took place. Parents, proud that their children were teaching, spread the news, and Tutorial Project staff members began making home visits.

In addition to the inter-grade tutoring by individual students, there is whole class tutoring where an entire older class visits a younger one, as well as intra-class tutoring in all grades.[41] Presently, grades 4–6 tutor students in grades K–3. In-service discussions about the learning and teaching processes are conducted by the teacher sending the tutors, using the Cross-Age Helping Program materials. The "receiving teacher" leads discussions, role plays, and simulations on specific subject matter. After tutoring sessions, both tutors and tutees evaluate their experiences, sometimes apart, sometimes with each other.

Evaluations through observation, questionnaires, and teachers' comments are as favorable as those reported by similar programs. Although neither pre- and post-test evaluations nor

40. "A Proposed Study to Develop a Tutorial Community in the Elementary School" (System Development Corporation, Santa Monica, California, 1968).

41. Gerald Newmark and Ralph J. Melaragno, "Tutorial Community Project: Report on the First Year (May, 1968–June, 1969)" (System Development Corporation, Santa Monica, California, n.d.); Ralph J. Melaragno and Gerald Newmark, "Tutorial Community Project: Report of the Second Year (July, 1969–August, 1970)," (System Development Corporation, n.d.).

comparison of experimental and control groups was undertaken, evaluative material was collected during the two years. In the second year kindergartners who were tutored as compared with those who had not received tutoring showed improved achievement, using eighteen learning goals established by kindergarten teachers and school marks as the comparative criteria.[42] The kindergarten teachers "reported that the kindergarten students received more individual attention and learned more in reading, writing and mathematics than had been true previously."[43] In describing how their classrooms, at the end of the year, differed from the past, the kindergarten teachers highlighted the following:

> More activities were going on at one time; more individual learning took place, with less group work; students had more choices among tasks and materials; the teachers were more aware of individual differences among the students, and had more time to work with individual students; there were fewer discipline problems, less bickering and fighting, and an increased willingness on the parts of the students to talk out their problems. Probably the idea that was expressed most forcefully was that the atmosphere in the classroom was much more relaxed and comfortable; this was true despite the fact that there were more people in the room, with a higher noise level.[44]

The marks of the twenty-two fifth-grade tutors were compared with those of all fifth-graders the previous school year.[45] Comparisons were made, for boys and girls separately, among the ten areas (seven cognitive and three affective) where marks were given. Of the twenty pairs of comparisons, the

42. Newmark and Melaragno, op. cit., pp. 28–31, tables 1–5. Melaragno and Newmark, op cit., pp. 16–17, tables 3–5.
43. Newmark and Melaragno, op cit., p. 33.
44. Ibid., p. 34.
45. No data are presented as to the comparability of the two groups, although it is the impression of the project directors that the twenty-two tutors were a representative sample of all fifth-graders. [Personal telephone conversation with Ralph Melaragno, September 17, 1970.]

pupils who tutored performed better on fourteen, as well on five, and less well on one.[46] And the twenty-two fifth-graders who tutored were present more often, absent and tardy less frequently than the average for the entire fifth the previous year.[47] While the data collection techniques do not permit of conclusive assertions, these findings appear to be corroborated by the tutors' teachers.

> Most teachers who sent tutors to the Kindergarten believed that their students had profited from the experience. They reported that some tutors had improved their attitudes toward school, in their behavior, and in their self-discipline. They also indicated that some tutors were able to carry over their experiences to their own classrooms, and helped their peers with school work.[48]

And outside evaluators who studied the Pocoima project reported that tutors liked to tutor and appeared to gain as a result; that kindergarten teachers "were convinced that the tutors had helped the Kindergarten students to learn"; that the sending teachers thought their pupils had learned.[49]

> Members of the Evaluation Team expressed strong feelings that the tutoring had been beneficial for the Kindergarten students, for the tutors, and for the Kindergarten teachers. While they felt that the tutoring was good, they stressed three problems: the need for more training and support for the tutors; the need for a different school organization that would allow time for planning and development of the tutorial system; and the need for a greatly increased involvement of parents so they would

46. Newmark and Melaragno, "Tutorial Community Project: Report . . . ," p. 32, tables 6–7. While similar data were not collected during the second year, it is the impression of the project directors that similar results obtained. [Personal visit, April 20, 1971.]

47. Ibid., p. 33, table 8. In a Berkeley, California, program tutors had absentee rates half that of a control group, and half again as low on tutoring days.

48. Ibid., p. 35.

49. Ibid., pp. 34 f.

know more about the Project and would be able to support it more.[50]

EACH ONE TEACH ONE

Less elaborate than the Pocoima effort is that taking place at P.S. 25, an elementary school in Yonkers, New York. Through the encouragement of the school superintendent, P.S. 25 undertook a school-wide Each One Teach One effort, in an attempt to improve learning and academic achievement through greater involvement of the pupils. During the summer of 1969 a group of teachers from the school met to draw up the objectives of the program, plan the structure, and write a booklet describing their decisions.

The organization of the program in its initial stages called for cross-graded instruction periods of varying lengths. Each classroom teacher drew up a master time-schedule chart. Children were scheduled to tutor and be tutored throughout the day with the exception of one hour in the morning. The classroom teachers were to set aside the last fifteen minutes each day for discussion and evaluation of Each One Teach One experiences. Problems of implementation have led to a more limited organization, moving toward pairing of teachers for tutorial arrangements, somewhat in the manner of Pocoima.

Goals of the program include skill development of both tutor and tutee; improvement of attitudes, confidence, and self-image; improved attitudes toward school; creation of relationships based on peer group ties and loyalties; provision of individualized and small group instruction; involvement of the community and parents in the school and improvement of

50. Ibid., p. 35. In Chapter V we will discuss how the Pocoima program has worked out some of these problems.

the relationship between the parents and the school; improvement of teachers' insight into the learning process, allowing them to delineate their roles more clearly.

The program was begun in September 1969. A questionnaire was administered to teachers in March 1970. These were some of the responses given to the question, "What are some of the successes you have encountered?"

In one discussion group I had a child call off six or seven methods of approaches which could be used with a student.

Another child having a great deal of difficulty in adding, teamed with a child with no idea of addition. The student made only little progress. However, the teacher (tutor) developed a mastery of the basic addition fact.

A very shy child now has a feeling of importance—participated in class more.

Children tutoring prefer to be called teachers.

Susan was a shy, withdrawn child with not much confidence. She began teaching Georgette and she now answers in class, and reminds me of EOTO time.

A boy who never had much interest in school, not only comes prepared for school, but takes out books for his "student" and wants to work with him at home.

I found the children are very disappointed if the person they are to work with happens to be absent.

A difficult child showed his best possible behavior when teaching a younger child to draw. A child with ability in arithmetic went to a classroom to tutor one child and gradually attracted a group of 7 or 8 to him and what he was doing.

LTT AT THE COLLEGE LEVEL

While all of the efforts described thus far have been with tutees at the elementary grade level and tutors from elementary through high school, the learning through teaching design is not intrinsically tied to any age or grade level. This is illustrated by the effort at Antioch College, where senior students in the physical sciences and engineering work with younger college students, and the work at McGill University in developing the "learning cell" design.

Seeking alternative methods to be used along with the lecture technique in large, undergraduate classes of 200 to 300 students, Marcel L. Goldschmid developed four strategic options including discussion, seminar, learning cell, and essay.[51] Students were able to choose the option most suitable for them for the duration of a half course on personality given in the fall (260 students) and repeated in the spring (160 students).

The learning-cell approach, according to Dr. Goldschmid, has been introduced at McGill by Donald Kingsbury, a mathematics lecturer. For the experiment it worked in the following way:

> Pairs of students were formed who interacted with each other during each of the two weekly one-hour sessions. The partners in the five to six dyads or cells rotated after each hour among a total group of ten to twelve students. This approach can take either of two forms: the two students in a cell can either

---

51. Marcel L. Goldschmid, "Instructional Options: Adopting the Large University Course to Individual Differences," *Learning and Development* 1, no. 5 (February 1970) (Center for Learning and Development, McGill University), p. 1.

both read the same material or choose different topics. In the first situation, student A asks his first question and student B attempts to answer and then asks his first question which student A will try to answer. What develops is a rather rapid flip-flop and intensive exchange between the two students throughout the hour. In the second alternative, student A first teaches the essence of his material to student B and then asks his questions. At the mid-point of the hour, they reverse their roles; student B presents his material and asks questions and student A tries to answer.[52]

From the pre-tests given to the students, including a personality test, an objective achievement test on course subject matter, and a questionnaire related to student backgrounds, no significant differences between students were shown. During the course students rated their feelings according to a 10-point "morale barometer."

The *average* ratings for the entire class on the 10-point scale ranged from 7.2 for the essay option to 8.2 for the learning cell option.[53]

All students completed a questionnaire subjectively evaluating important aspects of the course.

Peer and self evaluations of achievement were highest for the learning cell.[54]

When an unannounced essay examination was administered to all the students, the results showed that:

The students in the learning cell option achieved the highest scores on the unannounced essay examination. [Although] no significant differences were found between the four groups on

52. Ibid., p. 2.
53. Ibid., p. 3.
54. Ibid., p. 4.

the final [objective] examination which was independent of the work done in the four learning options.[55]

The several programs described above are major efforts in instituting learning through teaching in a single course, as at McGill; within a class or two, as in the Lippitts' efforts in Detroit; in a whole school, as in Pocoima, California, and Yonkers, New York; in an after-school program covering several schools, as in the New York City Homework Helper Program; and as part of a national program, with the National Commission on Resources for Youth, Youth Tutoring Youth programs.

There are a score or more descriptions of programs that bear mentioning in order to gain a better sense of the range and variety of these programs. Some focus upon children with special handicaps, as in the programs where "problem children" and "disabled" children are used as tutors, the program for "withdrawn" children, and the Maimonides learning rehabilitation clinic program. Other programs with classes composed of children of several ages (inter-age classes) use tutoring as part of the regular class activity. And in the Portland, Oregon, high schools, most of the children are engaged in an assisting program. Not only can tutoring aid both tutee and tutor, but as in the Hunter College program, it can be an important device in training teachers; it can also affect career decisions for youngsters. And the cross-age model has been transported to England, where the National Commission on Resources for Youth model is used to work with non-English-speaking Indian children. Of course, the Laubach Literacy programs in scores of countries are in essence learning through teaching programs.

55. Ibid.

In programs in which other principles are central, the idea of children teaching each other plays an important although less than central part, as in the British infant school design and the Micro-Social Pre-School Learning System.

LTT AND SLOW LEARNERS

Making the appeal to teachers of fifth and sixth grade more attractive by offering to accept their "problem children," a teacher of preprimary pupils who were not yet ready for first grade established a tutoring program at Santa Rosa, California.[56] Five tutors came in during three periods a day. A special tutoring corner was set up, and tutors worked with both individuals and small groups of students.

For junior high school students who had not learned basic elementary skills, tutoring was introduced "as a means of offsetting the stigma of relearning basic skills. . . ."[57] Underachieving seventh- and eighth-graders were enlisted to tutor children in two elementary schools.

> Primarily, the tutoring program was a motivational device used to encourage students to learn basic skills. Students thought that they "knew" how to do most of the skills taught in the primary and middle grades. They hesitated about learning primary-level reading and math skills for their own benefit, but they were willing to "relearn" such skills so that they might become tutors. In addition, the tutoring program

56. Letter, dated January 30, 1968, and Thermofaxed report, "Student-Tutor Program for First Graders" (n.d.), cited in Herbert Thelen, "Tutoring by Students: What Makes It So Exciting?" *The School Review* 77, no. 3 (September 1969): 229–244.

57. Katherine Van Wessem, "A Tutoring Program: The Second Year" (Brittany Junior High School, University City, Missouri, July 9, 1967), p. 10.

provided a means for building self-images of these disabled learners.[58]

Another project, also developed by the Central Midwestern Regional Educational Laboratory in Nashville, used a tutoring program "as a way to get (disabled) children to work at lower levels—to get them to do first and second grade work 'because they need first and second grade work.' "[59] As the program developed teachers found that the tutoring experience

built the self-concept of the tutor,

was a way to develop the tutor's academic skills,

created a need for tutors to learn social skills,

caused the tutor to analyze his learning process and to apply what he sees to his own learning style,

demanded role reversal and thus facilitated attitude changes toward school.[60]

In Lexington, Massachusetts, a sixth-grade science teacher, believing that "the learning difficulty of the slow learners is not a matter of degree, [rather that] slow learners learn differently,"[61] developed a program for her pupils to teach science

58. William R. Page, "Evaluation Report: The Tutoring Program" (Brittany Junior High School, University City, Missouri, July 9, 1967).

59. "Project Enable" (Cooperative project of the John F. Kennedy Center, George Peabody College for Teachers, Metropolitan Nashville School, Central Midwestern Regional Educational Laboratory, Model Cities Agency, Nashville, Tennessee, n.d.), p. 9.

60. Ibid., pp. 9 f. A similar program was used in a Lynnwood, Washington, elementary school to help "sixth graders, reading substantially below grade level, (by being) paired with three second graders who were almost non-readers." [Laura Rime and Jane Ham, "Sixth-Grade Tutors," *The Instructor* 77, no. 7 (March 1968): 104 f.]

61. Flores LeBoeuf, "*Qui Docet Discit*—He Who Teaches, Learns," *The Science Teacher* 35, no. 1 (January 1968): 55. The decision not to tutor within Lexington was based upon the belief that younger siblings and friends would be encountered and "the teaching role would be affected

to second-graders in Cambridge, Massachusetts. In a letter to parents of the sixth-graders, the teacher explained its assumptions as follows:

1. Eighth-graders will learn valuable scientific concepts in pursuing their role as science resource persons.

2. Eighth-graders will become more perceptive observers of the teaching-learning process; this new role will provide them with valuable insights into their own learning behavior and may enhance their ability in this area.[62]

"SPECIAL" CHILDREN

The use of students to aid others and themselves by teaching was used in another project involving "special" children. Children who were withdrawing from regular classroom work, who seldom paid attention during group lessons, and who very rarely completed their work had been placed in a special class. Using two of the class as "pupil-teachers," the entire class engaged in a program designed to improve reading. For those being taught, there was an increase in reading speed (ranging from 5 percent to 60 percent greater than anticipated).[63] And "both pupil-teachers made the greatest reading achievement gains (California Achievement Test). . . . With a five month interval between pre- and post-tests, the pupil-teachers made total reading gains of 1.4 and 2.6 years."[64]

---

and diluted by the relationships," and, despite the affluence of Lexington, many of the pupils had not traveled around the metropolitan Boston area.

62. Ibid., p. 54.

63. John Galvin and Mary Lynn Shoup, "The Use of Peers in Teaching Reading to Withdrawn Children" (U.S. Office of Education Grant G3-06-062063-1559 n.d.), p. 7 and table 1.

64. Ibid., pp. 7 f.

At the Maimonides Medical Center's learning rehabilitation clinic, New York City, staff encountered learning problems common to an environment of urban social disorganization.[65] Six first-grade children were identified as requiring special attention. Faced with a personnel squeeze, the staff decided that, if adequately trained, sixth-graders could act as teachers to the group of first-graders.

The sixth-grade children were chosen on the basis of teacher recommendations as to how well they could relate to younger children, not on academic achievement. Criteria included "capable of warm and accepting relationships with younger children."[66] The parents of the tutors were informed of the project and asked to grant permission for their children to participate.

Tutors were exposed to a daily, two-week training program. Training involved the learning of highly programmed specific tasks. The tutors became "experts" in these tasks, designed to overcome the development problems of the first-graders. They also participated in weekly evaluation meetings with the professional teachers. At the end of the school term the sixth-grade tutors helped to select and train fifth-graders to take their places the following year.

Although formal statistics were not gathered, success of the tutees was measured through observation by the principal, teacher, and Mental Health Center staff. Unfortunately, an even skimpier evaluation of tutor-derived benefits is mentioned.

65. Cecelia Pollack, Norman Sher, and Beatrice Teitel, "Child Helps Child and Both Learn" (Paper presented at the American Orthopsychiatric Association Annual Meeting, 1969).
66. Ibid., p. 3.

STUDENT ASSISTANTS

Nearly one-quarter of the two thousand students at Woodrow Wilson High School, Portland, Oregon, participate in the Student Assistant program. "[T]he kind of activities in which they were involved included large group presentations, small group presentations, individual tutoring, correction of homework, secretarial help in the office, operation of the Closed Circuit Television equipment, etc."[67] Unlike those efforts generated out of an academic concern, the Portland program

> developed out of a series of nagging concerns that young people of today were growing increasingly self-centered and materialistic, that the trend seemed to be for young people to become spectators rather than participants in the education process, that faculties and students needed to work closer together in a common goal of education, and that students seldom have the opportunity to be of service to someone else.[68]

The spirit that characterizes the Portland program is captured by Walter Rasmussen:

> Teenagers today are not needed—nothing is required of them. When our students volunteer to tutor young kids, they discover that somebody needs them as individuals. That's why they're willing to put in so much time and energy as tutors.[69]

Begun in 1965 in one school, the program has now spread nearly system wide. A unique feature here is the use of entire classes of older children who tutor a younger class one to

67. Personal letter from Principal William D. Proppe, December 27, 1967, cited in Thelen, "Tutoring by Students . . . ," p. 235.
68. Ibid.
69. Cited in *The Education Digest*, December 1969, p. 40.

three times a week for twenty to thirty minutes. The older children keep a log of their week; excerpts from two of them capture some of the flavor of the program:

> November 29. Sherry was stubborn and wouldn't work today. We are working on division. She doesn't try anymore.

> December 5. I don't know what to do about Sherry. She still won't try.

> December 9. All of a sudden Sherry understands division. She was pleasant and cooperative today. She was like she used to be. I guess I was wrong about her trying. She didn't understand and lost confidence. I am sorry I didn't understand the situation. She is a real good kid. I am never going to accuse her again.[70]

From another student's log:

> October 25. Kim still reads too fast.

> October 29. Today I devised a way to slow Kim down. If he reads aloud too fast, I give him a red strip of paper for a speeding ticket. If he reads with expression, I give him a green strip. We are going to make a graph of the strips and try to have it all green.

> November 25. Kim does better all the time. I swear he is smarter than me.[71]

INTER-AGE

Unlike the other efforts described—either cross-age or peer tutoring—in which children from one class tutor those in another, the Plainedge Schools on Long Island, New York,

---

70. J. Carl Fleming, "Pupil Tutors and Tutees Learn Together," *Today's Education* 58, no. 7 (October 1969): p. 48.
71. Ibid., p. 48.

have established "inter-age" classes with two- or three-year age spreads in one class. Designed to capitalize on the value of heterogeneity, a pupil constantly moves in and out of groups in some of which he knows more than others and in some less. There is, thus, a constant opportunity for cross-tutoring.[72]

And in La Grange, Illinois, problems of class size in the third, fourth, and fifth grades led to the establishment of a class consisting of eight third-graders, eight fourth-graders, and six fifth-graders. This multiage grouping "was found to be a natural setting for utilizing the helping relationship between older and younger children and age-mates within the group."[73] Because of the success of this initial effort, forced by circumstances in 1967, multiage groupings are being used in other elementary schools in the district.

TEACHER TRAINING

A variant on the notion that one learns through teaching is that one can learn to teach through teaching others to teach.[74] This notion has been incorporated in a program at Hunter College, New York City,[75] where college students in training to become teachers tutor ten-year-olds who in turn tutor seven-year-olds. "The college program was instituted to

72. Marie J. Yerry, "Interage Classes in the Plainedge (New York) School District," n.d.

73. Herbert A. Thelen, "Learning by Teaching" (Report of a Conference on the Helping Relationship in the Classroom, Stone-Brandel Center, University of Chicago, 1968), p. 36.

74. A further variant on this point is that playing a teaching role as a student will encourage the choice of teaching as a career. Citing more than a score of studies concerning the motivating factor(s) that led teachers to choose their profession, Wright makes an argument for allowing children to teach as a way to promote the supply of teachers. ["Should Children Teach?" passim.]

75. Similar programs are operating in Miami, Florida, and San Diego, California.

provide the college students with teaching experience with two different age levels of children, help them study teaching by acting as consultants to older children teaching younger children, and introduce them to the practice of encouraging youngsters to help each other learn."[76] Among the benefits cited for the program are

providing twice the number of children with tutoring aid;

boosting the self-esteem of the older children;

giving assistance to the regular classroom teachers;

providing the college students with a microcosmic learning situation and an active way to learn pedagogical principles.[77]

AN ENGLISH YOUTH TUTORING YOUTH EXPERIMENT

An English experiment drew upon the observation of Youth Tutoring Youth programs in America by the director of the Community Service Volunteers, Alec Dickson. In an area of Greater London largely populated by non-English-speaking Punjabees, a summer (1969) program was established with thirteen- to eighteen-year-old tutors working with six- to twelve-year-old tutees. The program, which ran for six weeks from 10:00 A.M. to 4:00 P.M., focused upon English language improvement. Among the results reported by the project director were the increased use of English for both the tutees and the tutors, a new status sense for the tutors, and a recog-

76. Elizabeth Hunter, "A Cross-Age Tutoring Program Encourages the Study of Teaching in a College Methods Course," *Journal of Teacher Education* 19, no. 4 (Winter 1968): 449.

77. Ibid.; "10-Year-Olds Are Tutoring 7-Year-Olds," *Education News* (January 22, 1968), p. 8.

nition by the community of a voluntary out-of-school program.[78]

Although the prime focus of the British infant schools is concerned with "discovery" learning, aspects of children teaching each other are important to the program. According to an unpublished study conducted by Bethanie L. Gilbert for Westinghouse Learning Corporation, discovery learning

> . . . makes every child an independent, autonomous human being, interacting with similar human beings, whether 2 feet or 5 and a half feet tall. It also makes every person (even an unsuspecting visitor) a potential resource for knowledge and information. Thus, approval, control, and responsibility are no longer exclusively centered in the teacher. Other children, materials, and any adult who happens to be handy, serve as equally important sources of information and "reinforcement." . . . The amount of interaction among the children seems to take tremendous pressure off the teachers. . . . In each school, a staff lounge would be filled at tea time, with perhaps one teacher and one or two ancillary staff or volunteer parents with the children. Meanwhile, the children would be putting each other to nap . . .

As in the "inter-age" programs described above, the infant schools group together children of several ages, usually five through seven. This "family grouping" gives special support to the young child as he enters the strange new world of the school. The emotional benefits are primary, although the opportunities for peer learning are evident.

78. Hugh Anderson, "The Southall Project" (Youth Tutors Youth, A C/S/V report, Community Service Volunteers, London, England, n.d.), pp. 31 f.

LEARNING WITH PARTNERS

The Micro-Social Pre-School Learning System, an elementary school readiness program developed by Dr. Myron Woolman, provides another example in which children teaching each other is integral to the program but not the essential focus. Most of the children involved in the preschool program located in a center in Vineland, New Jersey, are from low-income migrant families. In the Woolman system the teacher becomes the planner and organizer. The most important aspect of the program is the materials; they become the real teacher.

To generate language learning, accelerate communication, and reduce the teacher's load, children work in pairs helping each other to learn, reviewing and checking each other's work. In fact, the helping process has carried over into the simulated play areas, where the children elect to work together.

Not only do children work in pairs, but each child also assumes the role of a monitor, helping the children who have not progressed to the point where he is, either because they entered a particular learning module at a later point or because they work more slowly. Functioning as a monitor enables the child to review and reperceive his work and to learn skills for helping other people learn. The monitoring system is highly structured, and children do not participate in a random fashion. Initially the children felt that they were wasting time; now their attitudes are quite positive as they experience success and really do learn. In fact, at the end of the school year, when the children who had participated in the Micro-Social School were being prepared for the "regular" school they would attend in the fall, their prime concern was whether they would continue "learning with partners."

51

We have described effects upon and benefits both to the tutor and tutee. Traditional notions of teaching/learning would suggest that in such a transaction one party gives and the other receives. We have suggested that this need not be the case—both tutor and tutee can benefit, and gain to each derives from the interaction between the two. The relationship is, in a sense, symbiotic.

> The tutee feels that with his tutor's help he can learn to read (he is *my* tutor) and the tutor learn reading techniques because he has to be successful (with *my* tutee) in the process.[79]

The tutor and the tutee do not benefit alike—they each benefit but in different ways. And from the data it appears that the tutor may benefit in a greater number of ways, as a greater number of mechanisms appear to be tapped by the process of tutoring.

79. Jack Hassinger and Murray Via, "How Much Does a Tutor Learn Through Teaching Reading," *Journal of Secondary Education* 44, no. 1 (January 1969): 43.

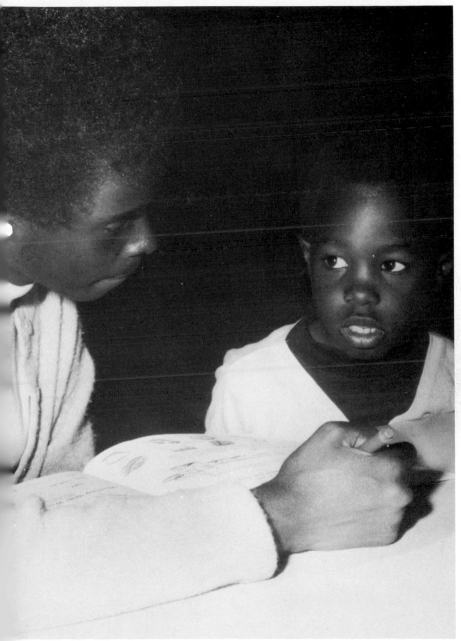

John Valdez, Jr.

Gisella Hoelcl

Don Pettersen

John Valdez, Jr.

July 12, 1967

Elizabeth Avenue

They don't keep it clean. The sweeping man has to get up early in the morning and sweeps the streets and when he turns around the papers is right back on the streets. Nobody picks up papers even when a basket is next to them.

The park is nice and green and the branches are in good health. The flowers are nice and lovely when the boys don't pick them.

Men when they are drinking beer they throw their cans into the green lively grass and it look like a dump truck.

The boys climb the trees and let the limb fall down on the green grass and

never picks them up.

I went to a park on 4 of July and it was nice and clean they had a sign - boys keep out but they still comes in there and mess it up.

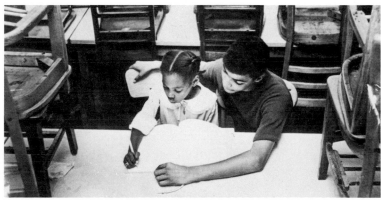

Len Gordon

CHAPTER III

I went through it [quantum theory] once and looked up only to find the class full of blank faces— they had obviously not understood. I went through it a second time and they still did not understand it. And so I went through it a third time, and that time I understood it.[1]

How It Works: The Mechanisms

Programs of children teaching other children involve a variety of processes—most immediately those affecting the child doing the teaching and the child being taught. Before turning to the main focus of this chapter—a discussion of the mechanisms whereby learning through teaching affects the tutor—let us briefly note the ways in which the child being taught may be affected, as well as the potential effect upon the adult teacher and the school.

FOR THE TUTEE

From the point of view of the child being taught, perhaps the two key factors are the greater "closeness" of the child

1. Jerome Bruner, *The Process of Education* (New York: Vintage Books, 1963), pp. 88 f.

as teacher as compared with the adult teacher, and the individualization of attention.[2]

This "closeness" may be no more than a matter of age, but it may also involve sex, race, or background. Further, if we are to accept Bruner's notion that "the task of teaching a subject to a child at any particular age is one of representing the structure of that subject in terms of the child's way of viewing things,"[3] it may be that being "closer" to his fellows, the child as teacher may better understand another "child's way of viewing things." Or, to go a step further with Bruner, "Of course, it may be that nothing is intrinsically difficult. We just have to wait until the proper point of view and corresponding language for presenting it are revealed."[4] Again, it may be that another child is more likely to have that "point of view" and to speak that "language." And, in a sense, the underachieving older child "has been there," and can have greater empathy with and understanding for the younger child who is not achieving.

Individualization involves special attention, explanation, immediate and direct feedback, and personalization.[5] Style and

2. These factors are far from precise. We should expect no more, however, because as the summary report of a conference on the effect of teachers notes, "*at the present moment we cannot make any sort of meaningful quantitative estimate of the effect of teachers on student achievement.*" [Alexander M. Mood, "Do Teachers Make a Difference?" in *Do Teachers Make a Difference?: A Report on Recent Research on Pupil Achievement* (Washington, D.C.: U.S. Office of Education, 1970), p. 7 (italics in the original).]

3. Bruner, *The Process of Education*, p. 33.

4. Ibid., p. 40.

5. A unique program in Westport, Connecticut, used those third-graders who had previous music training to teach music notation to classmates who had not had such lessons. The group taught this way did better on tests than those taught by the teacher, "the students who had higher achievement skill in note-reading gained status in the eyes of their peers; the less musically able children gained confidence as their skills increased; and music study seemed to gain standing as an academic subject." [Renee B. Fisher, "An Each One–Teach One Approach to Music Notation," *Grade Teacher* 86, no. 6 (February 1969): 120]

content of the material to be learned is adjusted to the individual being taught. One may say that the material and the way it is taught are put in the special idiom of the learner. These factors provide not only the direct attention to the particular needs of the child, but also, because of the fact of the special attention, are likely to encourage a sense of importance and self-esteem upon the part of the child receiving this special attention. However, when all children are made a part of such programs, the power of the special attention is, of course, reduced, and other factors must be sought to give power to the program.

In addition to the factors of "closeness" and individualization, the child who is being taught by another child gains from the opportunity to imitate or model himself after the other child. This may be simply a matter of a child being better able to envision himself becoming like another child, as compared with the far older and more distant teacher, or it may be a much closer modeling if the other child is alike in race and/or sex and/or ethnicity and/or background.

Bronfenbrenner, in his comparative study of children in the United States and the U.S.S.R., cites a number of studies relating to the power of modeling. He concludes, "involving persons actually or potentially important to the child in pursuit of a superordinate goal can have the effect of maximizing the incidence and inductive power of constructive behaviors and motives while reducing disruptive and negative influences."[6]

Noting that American children are more likely to look to their peers as opposed to adults for models, as contrasted to the Soviet children, Bronfenbrenner states, "The most needed innovation in the American classroom is the involvement of

6. Urie Bronfenbrenner, *The Two Worlds of Childhood: U.S. and U.S.S.R.* (New York: Russell Sage Foundation, 1970), pp. 148 f.

pupils in responsible tasks on behalf of others within the class-room, the school, the neighborhood, and the community."[7]

WHAT'S IN IT FOR THE TEACHER

For teachers whose pupils either teach or are taught by other children, there are various possible benefits. The teacher's role may expand from one of sole dispenser of knowledge to include that of resource person, manager of learning, or orchestrator of various teaching-learning activities. Teachers whose younger students are helped by older tutors gain such benefits as:

A. The knowledge that their diagnostic and creative skills are being used to provide individual attention that they themselves don't have time to give.

B. Satisfaction from making an important contribution to the education of the older students who are working with them.

C. More time and energy to devote to the needs of their other students.[8]

When the teachers are involved in training feedback sessions with children who teach others, there is the opportunity for the adult teacher to observe the process of teaching. This factor is central to Dr. Hunter's program (see Chapter II), in which college students in training to become teachers gain insight into the teaching process by working with sixth-grade youngsters who in turn will be tutoring younger children. The opportunity to observe, monitor, and affect the teaching of another offers the potentiality for gaining deeper insight into the teaching process. As the supervisor of a program using

7. Ibid., p. 156.
8. Lippitt, Eiseman, and Lippitt, *Cross-Age Helping Program* . . . , p. 12.

junior high school youngsters to tutor elementary grade children noted in reporting upon the tutors' observations based upon their own teaching: "Their acute awareness of what prevents learning caused the [adult] program teachers to be even more concerned about their own teaching techniques."[9]

Where there is a practice of pairing classes for the purpose of establishing tutorial teams, as in Pocoima, the two adult teachers have an opportunity to plan and work together, something largely absent in the traditional self-contained classroom.

Finally, it is likely that having been teachers, the children will themselves bring new characteristics to their role as pupils. While this may in some instances be threatening—the child knows too much or too many of the "tricks of the trade"—surely the adult teacher can see in the pupil who has been a teacher someone with new strengths and insight who can be a more effective learner, a more challenging pupil, for that experience.

For the school where children are teachers, there are likely to be many changes in climate—not merely the structuring and restructuring required by the program (see Chapter V), but more basically the new way in which children will come to see themselves and the consequences for the school. A child who has been given the responsibility of teaching another child is less likely to tolerate some of the demeaning aspects of school procedure, such as passes, hall monitors, and trivial regulations. Although sure to be a long way from the notion of a community of scholars of the medieval University of Paris, a school of children who are teachers will likely be one that is less rigid and hierarchical, or, at least, one in which rigidity and hierarchy are more likely to be challenged. Also, in a school where children carry some of the responsibility

9. Van Wessem, "A Tutoring Program: The Second Year," p. 11.

for its central business, teaching/learning, identification with it and its goals may increase, perhaps even to the level associated with the "school spirit" that currently is attracted only to interscholastic sports.

COGNITIVE BENEFITS FOR THE TUTOR

The effects upon the child who is taught, the adult teacher, and the school are each important and of consequence to the establishment of programs where children teach other children. However, it is the central concern of this chapter to examine the mechanisms involved in affecting the child who learns as a consequence of teaching another. An overview of these factors can be gleaned from an evaluator's report on the Pocoima program.

I asked everyone I interviewed what changes they had seen in the children who are tutors. From the parents came the response that they had noticed that they no longer were having trouble with their grades. From the tutors themselves, they nearly all said that they now understand how a teacher feels, they understand how a student feels, and that they are more understanding of the teaching/learning process. One curious thing that came up again and again, from the tutors, was that they said that one of the gains was that the things they had missed in kindergarten or first grade came up and they had to learn them for the first time. Such things as alphabetical order, number concepts, reading, singing, memorizing, etc., and particularly the rules of behavior and how much of a problem is created when the learner is not attending. Nearly all the tutors learned this from being teachers for a while. When I asked if they thought the classes could get along without them, they said no, that they needed them now, that there were things that they couldn't do in class when they were without tutors being present and this gives them a feeling of being needed, being important and this is verified by the teachers that I interviewed.[10]

Analytically, one can conveniently divide these mechanisms between the cognitive and the emotional. Under the cognitive area we will address the ways in which the child as teacher both learns more, as well as learns about learning. Under the emotional, we will consider the emotional, social, and psychological factors that appear to be involved. While analysis is abetted by this division, the two factors are not in fact separate, as the cognitive and affective domains are combined in the experience of the child.

Jerome Bruner has cited the experience of a college teacher of physics introducing an advanced class to the quantum theory.[11] The simple notion of knowing/learning as a result of teaching can be broken down into various parts. Initially, one can divide those aspects which have to do with specific subject matter from more generic learning.

Learning by Reviewing

In the process of teaching another, one may review material already learned and thus grasp it more fully or deeply. A study of the Learning Assistants program at the Cherry Creek School District, Colorado, reports that the high school students who taught science to elementary school children found that doing so *reinforced* science concepts previously learned. This is in contradistinction to seeing in such a process the opportunity to learn something new; in addition the Cherry Creek high school students did feel that participating in the

10. Cited in Newmark and Melaragno, "Tutorial Community Project: Report . . . ," p. 96.
11. Bruner, *The Process of Education*, pp. 88 f.

program also stimulated them to learn more about science.[12] The process of reinforcing already learned knowledge itself has several dimensions. The child uses or works with the material several times: first, when initially learning it, perhaps some years ago; second, in reviewing it; third, in preparing it to teach to another; and, finally, in presenting it to the other child. And it is not only a simple matter of reviewing the material; in doing so one may reperceive it, may see it in new ways, perhaps synthesize it into new formulations, enriching one's knowledge of that material as well as material subsequently learned.

Another aspect of learning the substance of a subject by teaching it is suggested by Clark Abt's proposal for the use of games as a teaching tool.[13] He suggests a variety of games, each of which basically involves a child checking another to see if he is correct. Perhaps somewhat richer in its possibilities for learning is Woolman's use of children to monitor others in his Micro-Social Pre-School Learning System. The key role here is the child monitoring another to be sure the first child has learned the material. For the monitor, of course, there is the chance to review the material.

In learning by teaching, the child who is teaching finds a meaningful use for the subject, a use that goes beyond his own self, a utility for his knowledge. One may even call it a social use of knowledge. Related to this is the experience of many tutors that their new role demands their learning more or understanding the subject better in order to fulfill the expectations of the child who is being taught. The under-

12. Eighty-three percent of the high school students felt that participating in the program reinforced science concepts previously learned, while 69 percent felt it stimulated them to learn more about science. [Diana Norton, "The 'Mutually Aided Learning' Project as Seen by the High School 'Learning Assistants,'" (Cherry Creek Schools, Englewood, Colorado, n.d.).]

13. Clark Abt, *Serious Games* (New York: Viking Press, 1970), p. 42.

achieving child placed in the teaching role is now given responsibility that may call upon him to strive mightily in order to meet this challenge.

We have implicitly assumed, up to now, that the child in the teaching role already "knows" the subject matter, that in the process of teaching he learns more of it or understands it better or more richly, while the child being taught does not know the material. However, one can develop, as at McGill University, a learning through teaching design when neither student knows the particular material and they both can seek it out.[14]

A variant on this is for a Spanish-speaking child to teach that language to an English-speaking tutee as a way for each to learn both Spanish and English. "The Spanish-speaking children in order to teach their language to an English-speaker, must acquire an increasing knowledge of English in order to communicate with their classmates."[15] Of course, such a design also gives status and pride to the Spanish speaker in that he has something to give, it teaches both children that Spanish is as accepted a language as English, and it teaches the English-speaking child a foreign language. And finally, for the Spanish-speaking tutor to teach in Spanish leads to a retention of that language and a building of fluency and literacy in it.

Learning by Reformulation

As we have mentioned before, the process of preparing material in order to teach another involves not only a review of the material but also may lead the child as teacher to re-

14. See Chapter II; also *Learning and Development I*, no. 5 (February 1970); 1, no. 8 (May 1970) (Center for Learning and Development, McGill University).

15. Frank Riessman and Frank Alberts, "Digging 'The Man's' Language," *Saturday Review* (September 17, 1966), p. 98.

formulate the material, organize the facts in a new way, even seek out the structure or basic character of the material. Thus, already knowing the "facts" of the subject, the child as teacher may be better able to grasp the underlying structure; indeed, the challenge of teaching another may require doing just that.

Surely the child in teaching another will seek out examples, analogies, illustrations, all as ways to teach better. In addition, as Bruner has stated, "Mastery of the fundamental ideas of a field involves not only the grasping of general learning, but also the development of an attitude toward learning and toward guessing and hunches, toward the possibility of solving problems on one's own."[16]

The child who teaches another child and thereby learns himself, not only has to struggle to make the material meaningful to the learner, but also has the opportunity of observing another in the process of learning, perhaps leading him to reflect upon his own learning process. "Tutors often related their own prior failures and spoke about changes they could make in their own learning styles."[17] This opportunity may increase his awareness of the patterns of learning, for in order to teach another he may need to call upon his own experiences in learning and how he learned. This process may lead to seeing problems in new and different ways, to reformulate them, to reconceptualize issues, or as Bruner puts it: "To learn structure, in short, is to learn how things are related."[18]

In the cognitive area, then, the child having taught another may himself learn as a result of a number of processes. *He reviews the material; he has to organize, prepare, illustrate the material to present it to his student; he may try to reshape or reformulate it so as to enable his pupil to learn it and thus*

16. Bruner, *The Process of Education*, p. 28.
17. Van Wessem, "A Tutoring Program: The Second Year," p. 13.
18. Bruner, *The Process of Education*, p. 7.

himself sees it in new ways; he may need to seek out the basic character of the subject, its structure, in order to teach it better, and may thereby himself understand it better.

Observing another learn and trying to attune his teaching so as to further another's learning gives the teacher insight into the general learning process and perhaps better enables the teacher to learn when he is again in the pupil role. In other words, not only may a child learn from the act of teaching, but having been a teacher he may then be a better learner when he again becomes a pupil. And perhaps further, this moving back and forth between teacher and pupil roles, with learning taking place in both, may provide a quantum leap in the amount of learning that occurs. Another aspect of this was captured by a sixth-grade tutor in a California program:

> When my teacher does something that I think is bad teaching, I ask myself now how would I do it. Then I make myself my own teacher, and I teach myself the better way.[19]

If it is true that one can learn through teaching, or even further, if teaching is the ultimate learning activity, then a school where every pupil is a teacher truly becomes a learning institution.

SOCIAL AND EMOTIONAL BENEFITS

Programs of children teaching may not only lead to direct cognitive effect but may also have emotional, social, and psychological impact that in turn may affect cognitive growth, as well as having benefit in and of itself. Perhaps the most direct effect has to do with the building of self-respect, ego strength, among the children who teach. For example, a

19. "Pint-Size Tutors Learn by Teaching," *American Education* (April 1967), p. 29.

study of the Beaverton, Oregon, program reports: "One boy consciously carried his tutoring materials so his third grade math book would be obvious to his junior high school peers. When they asked him why he was only doing third grade math, he proudly informed them that he taught third grade at an elementary school."[20] This may be especially important for those youngsters who have not experienced great success in school but who, nonetheless, as in Youth Tutoring Youth and other programs, are placed in the teacher or tutor role.[21] This new role with its ascription of special and high status offers powerful incentive to children.[22] It can lead not only to self-confidence of personality—note Bruner's comment that such can be merely "the self-confidence of fools"[23]—but also the self-confidence of mastery, or responsibility, of knowing a subject.

Upon examination, learning through teaching programs reveal some of the facets of self-confidence itself.[24] One might

20. Van Wessem, "A Tutoring Program: The Second Year," p. 6.

21. To the extent that tutoring leads to positive identity with teachers, it may also profit pupils. See Virgil Pinckney, "The Teacher, Delinquent, and the Training School," *Michigan Education Journal* 11 (January 1963): 356. And, conversely, to the extent teachers perceive pupils who tutor as successful students, it may be of further value to the student. See Robert Rosenthal and Lenore Jacobson, *Pygmalion in the Classroom: Teacher Expectation and Pupil's Intellectual Development* (New York: Holt, Rinehart and Winston, 1968).

22. Bottom notes Moreno's finding (Jacob L. Moreno, *Psychodrama* [New York: Beacon House, 1966]) that "the position of children's image in the eyes of their peers was enhanced when jobs were assigned that held status in the eyes of their class members." [Raymond Bottom, "The Effect of Tutorial Experiences on Pupil Tutor and Tutored Pupil in Intelligence, Achievement and Social-Psychological Adjustment in Twenty Culturally Deprived Children" (Monroe, Michigan, Public Schools, n.d.).]

23. Bruner, *The Process of Education*, p. 65.

24. There is considerable literature as to the importance of self-concept in learning. See, for example, Eugene L. Hartley and Ruth Hartley, *Outside Readings in Psychology* (New York: Thomas Y. Crowell, 1957), pp. 250 ff.; Mary Jean Klucive, "Self-Image and the First-Grade Pupil," in *Ginn and Company Contributions in Reading* 23 (1964); Joseph Bledsoe

separate out three aspects: the factor of being singled out, specially chosen; the doing of an important activity; and the developing of competence. When all children are involved, as they might be in a fully developed learning through teaching program, the aspect of being singled out, uniqueness—a status characteristic—becomes less important and the emphasis turns to more functional factors, the meaningfulness of the effort and the competence acquired. And a century ago, William Bentley Fowle pointed out the value of involving all the children in both the tutor and pupil roles. "The monitorial plan, as I used it, is the true democratic one: the children all had a chance at the offices. . . . Being sometimes governed, children are less likely to become imperious; and sometimes commanding, they will not easily become servile."[25] And Bronfenbrenner points out that "if a special program is confined to an isolated classroom, it . . . also risks the danger that the rest of the school, especially children in other classes, will perceive the 'special class' in invidious terms . . . and treat its members accordingly."[26]

The relationship between self-confidence and cognitive growth is complicated. It has generally been assumed that self-confidence leads to, permits, is enabling toward cognitive proficiency. This formulation would seem to undergird the National Commission on Resources for Youth program, as well as the work of Thelen, and to be corroborated by the

and Karl G. Garrison, "The Self-Concept of Elementary School Children in Relation to Their Academic Achievement, Intelligence, Interests, and Manifest Anxiety" (U.S. Office of Education Cooperative Research Project No. 1008); Percy V. Williams, "School Dropouts," *NEA Journal* 52, no. 2 (February 1963); William Brookover, Thomas Shailes, and Ann Peterson, "Self-Concept of Ability and School Achievement," *Sociology of Education* 37, no. 3 (Spring 1964): 271–278; Bottom, "The Effect of Tutorial Experiences . . . ," pp. 4–9.

25. Fowle, *The Teacher's Institute*, p. 193.

26. Bronfenbrenner, *The Two Worlds of Childhood: U.S. and U.S.S.R.*, p. 158.

evidence of the "Coleman Report."[27] Bruner may be suggesting that the acquisition of cognitive knowledge leads to enhanced self-confidence. One might synthesize these approaches and say that the acquisition of cognitive knowledge enhances self-confidence, which in turn encourages the acquisition of further cognitive knowledge.

This self-confidence, the gaining of ego strength, may have a special character, having been the result of helping another, growing out of a cooperative relationship. The way in which one builds ego strength, just as the way in which one learns, may have effect upon how one grows and learns in the future. Having developed strength by and learning from helping another, as contrasted with doing so at the expense of another, may lead the individual to see self-growth and individual learning as part of a cooperative collegial relationship, not necessarily one of competition or at the expense of another.[28]

The sense of self-accomplishment can give the child as teacher new confidence and new responsibility, and can lead to new interests. In this last regard, Benjamin Wright, who surveyed the causal factors involved in leading people to choose teaching as a career, found that prior teaching experience played a central role.[29] And it is easy to speculate as to the many other career options, in addition to public school teaching, that are revealed by involving children in helping others. To be sure, having taught, the child may

27. James Coleman, *Equality of Educational Opportunity* (Washington, D.C.: U.S. Office of Education, 1966).

28. Note on this point Abt's suggestion that children perceive "grading on a curve" as instinctively unfair and realize that their doing well has the consequence of "making things tough for the others." He suggests a marking system that is not a zero-sum game but rather one in which success is achieved in a more socially cooperative way, with groups of students striving toward an objective achievement goal. [Abt, *Serious Games*, p. 24.]

29. Wright, "Should Children Teach?" p. 353.

well decide he does not want to become a teacher, as the story told by a child in Atlanta points out. "After teaching two tutees, I know how it must feel with a room full. I enjoyed being a tutor, but I wouldn't want to be a teacher." Surely it is better for the child to have had a tryout at teaching than to go with the field only to discover too late his lack of interest.

The effect of teaching others upon the youngster who is teaching may be as simple as overcoming shyness, changing the reticence of a loner.

I had a problem once; I was shy, too, like she [the tutee] is and we both tried to bring each other out.[30]

I learned how to get along with people younger than myself and older, also I can practically talk to anyone, which is quite a change for me, because I just don't have anything to say to strangers, no matter how old they are.[31]

Thelen places special emphasis upon the emotional effect upon pupils.[32] Not only does the child gain new interests, but he may become better adjusted, more adequate as a person, attain better character. Thelen emphasizes that when this occurs in programs such as those we are discussing, the result may be to decrease the self-centered and materialistic orientation of the children and to change them from spectators (pupils) to participants (teachers). Many observers of such programs have remarked on the changes in the tutor—a greater sense of responsibility, especially as it relates to another; a greater maturity, seriousness of purpose; a better understand-

30. Jeffrey Eiseman and Peggy Lippitt, "Olders-Youngers Evaluation: Covering the First Semester" (Report to the Stern Family Fund and the Detroit Public School, Center for Research on Utilization of Scientific Knowledge, University of Michigan, February 1966), p. 7.
31. Ibid., p. 16.
32. Thelen, "Tutoring by Students . . . ," passim.

ing of individual differences. And given the opportunity to play a variety of roles, both subordinate and superordinate, the child thereby may be better prepared to occupy the variety of roles found in our increasingly complex adult society.

In the work on cross-age projects of Peggy and Ronald Lippitt and their colleagues, special emphasis has been placed upon the socialization process.

> One assumption underlying our pilot projects has been that much of the process of socialization involves use by the younger children of the behavior and attitudes of older children as models for their own behavior.
>
> A second assumption of our projects has been that involvement of older children in a collaborative program with adults to help younger children will have a significant socialization impact on the older children because of (1) the important motivational value of a trust-and-responsibility-taking relationship with adults around a significant task, and (2) the opportunity to work through—with awareness but at a safe emotional distance—some of their own problems of relationships with their siblings and peers.[33]

Cross-age helping can, they say, serve to build a peer group attitude that supports the value of helping youngsters, and can allow the helpers to "discover alternative ways of being influential other than coercion or rebellion."[34] As to relations with siblings, a training seminar leader in a Detroit project reported that "some [children] told me their younger brothers and sisters stopped being so obnoxious to them and started being human again."[35] And an older tutor said:

> I have a sister 7 and a nephew 9, two nieces, one 4, the other 4

33. Lippitt and Lohman, "Cross-Age Relationships . . . ," p. 114.
34. Lippitt, Eiseman, and Lippitt, *Cross-Age Helping Program* . . . , p. 111.
35. Eiseman and Lippitt, "Olders-Youngers Evaluation . . . ," p. 13.

months. I feel that now I have an understanding of their behavior, problems, and abilities.[36]

This effect is seen not only by teachers and the students
but by a tutor's mother:

We were thinking last year of moving to a nicer neighborhood,
but I decided against it. I was afraid Debbie wouldn't get this
opportunity in another school. That girl has never been so
contented, and I know it's just because she has the chance of
helping another person. After Debbie began tutoring, she'd
come home every day all excited about what she'd taught that
day to Patricia. Then she'd start planning next day's lessons.
She made us set up a back room in the house as her school-
work room. My husband worried that taking time to teach
someone else might make Debbie's marks go down. But they've
gone up. She used to be N in arithmetic—"that means Needs
Improvement." Now she gets G.[37]

Where the children teaching and being taught are different
in terms of age, sex, race, cultural background, or ethnic
group, the relationship may serve to reduce barriers based
upon these factors. The teacher-to-student relationship puts
the child as teacher in a new relationship to another child,
and depending upon how the program is structured, in a new
relationship with that pupil's adult teacher. Also, having
taught, the child as teacher now has shared a key experience
with his own teacher, a factor that may lead to new relationships in his own classroom. Teaching may be both demystified
and raised in respect as a consequence.

The child who is a teacher comes to play a role of responsibility and leadership as part of a helping relationship, in a
way where the pair of children can come to develop a com-

36. Ibid., p. 14.
37. "Pint-Size Tutors Learn by Teaching," p. 29.

mon purpose while at the same time a bond can be developed between the child as teacher and the adult teacher.

In reporting the results of a conference addressed to the key question, "Do Teachers Make a Difference?" the chairman, Alexander Mood, concludes that "the students must be integral elements of the organizational enterprise. . . . To this end all children must regularly be assigned teaching roles."[38] Among the several factors underlying this strong recommendation, Dr. Mood calls attention to the fact that "education is more and more becoming lifelong as technology accelerates and much of it will necessarily take place on the job and in the home so that all of us will be continually teachers and learners."[39] And as preparation for their roles as parents, particularly in light of the recognition of the importance of the child's preschool years, Dr. Mood suggests "that all students must be taught to lead their own children effectively through those first years . . ."[40]

The variety of learning situations in which students can help each other is limited only by the participants' imaginations, as this list of thirteen suggests:

1. One-to-one tutoring.

2. One tutor with a group of tutees.

3. A student acting as teacher with small group or entire class.

4. A student acting as "buddy" or "big brother" to another student.

5. A student acting as a "listening board" for another student.

38. Mood, "Do Teachers Make a Difference?" p. 16.
39. Ibid., p. 39.
40. Ibid., p. 39.

6. A student giving reassurance to another student, sometimes merely by presence.

7. A student giving approval or praise to other students for tasks accomplished.

8. Friend or companion to another student while on a field trip, during lunch periods, recess breaks, or on the playground.

9. Student leader of interest groups or clubs.

10. Fellow reader with another student.

11. Teams of students at the same level, working on the same task.

12. Student library aides who help other students find and use materials.

13. One-to-one helping teams in lab or shop situations.[41]

We have examined some of the processes whereby children can gain both cognitively and emotionally as a result of teaching other children. To say that children *can* gain from this process is not to say that it *will* happen. A program of children teaching other children can fail, it can be denied by the too-common proclivity of school bureaucracy toward robbing the fresh and inventive of their life. It can become a program of reward for the "smart" child and come to be seen by the "dumb" as an imposition, or children can be "forced" to tutor, or it can be a way for a school to seek to replace paid staff with pupils (as happened to the Lancaster program). Tutors can teach the tutee things that are wrong, or teach him in a harmful way. Teachers, trained to teach, may either feel not capable of managing and supervising a tutoring program or feel threatened by a successful tutor, or both. For success to come about, for the program to tap the potential for

41. Herbert A. Thelen, "Learning by Teaching," pp. 17 ff.

both cognitive and emotional gain for the child as teacher (as well as for the child being taught), the processes involved need to be identified and understood. This chapter has sought to do that, while the next chapter illustrates the steps necessary for successful implementation.

CHAPTER IV

Youth Tutoring Youth: From Demonstration to Implementation

The Youth Tutoring Youth program of the National Commission on Resources for Youth, perhaps more than any other tutoring program of its scope, is concerned primarily with the tutor's learning and development. From its inception the basic target population of YTY has been the disadvantaged Neighborhood Youth Corps youngsters who are underachieving in the schools. *Because this after-school program accents tutor development, the learning through teaching concept can attain fullest significance.* The entire design reflects this emphasis; it is present in such aspects as the pre-service and in-service training of the tutor, the orientation provided for the supervisors and administrators of the program, and the way materials are developed.

The YTY program is based upon a powerful respect for the

unutilized inner resources of disadvantaged youngsters. The model is rooted in role theory. By placing the underachieving adolescent in the role of the helper, tutor, giver, his own power can be developed and released, his image of himself changed, the images held of him by other people changed, his competency increased, new resources developed. YTY adds to this process its entire training and management focus, which is directed toward reinforcing the role. By having the tutors develop games, construct curricula, and make decisions, YTY further enhances what is natural to the role.

The tutoring role itself, by the very nature of the relationship between the tutor and the tutee, brings forth a new responsibility. Unlike the "responsibility" given in school for erasing the blackboard, the tutor is placed in a position of being responsible for the learning of another. He is implicitly told, "This child is in your charge and *you have something to give*. If you didn't have something to give, we would never have put you in this position." For the tutee comes the reward of receiving attention from an older youngster, a coveted moment for a younger child and yet unheard of to most of them. The tutee not only has an older youngster paying attention to him, but actually working with him, listening, sharing his experiences.

There is a big difference between YTY, which is an after-school program, and the regular school. Most of the things youngsters learn in school are things that have very little to do with them—the stars, the moon, people of other lands. About the only time the person himself becomes legitimate for study is when he gets into trouble; then his behavior, his life outside school, his problems are inquired into. "Now, what's troubling you?" the counselor asks. But until then the self has been irrelevant as content. In YTY youngsters investigate the environment that is closest to them—themselves. The aim is to let learning spring from themselves out, rather than from the outside world in.

Most of the suggestions and exercises used in the training of the tutor (and the tutee) are those that will lead to engaging the youngster in *his own content as the starting point of instruction.* He begins to study about himself, his likes, his feelings, his sensations, and the way he sees the community around him. This is very different from what people generally think of tutoring, namely that each tutee learns to read better or to pass tests. Most people, including the young tutors, have been conditioned to adopt this traditional notion of tutoring. Even a very young child in playing school has internalized this notion so that his tutoring consists of mimicking the teacher, in such ways as "Sit down, open your book, take out your pencil." The conceptions of what school should be—never fun—have been deeply ingrained into the youngsters who come to the YTY program. YTY trainers say, "Look! there are a lot of things you can teach your tutee about reading and other skills through using what he has going for him, using his own interest as a staging point of instruction."

The YTY program endeavors to improve the self-definition of the learners, both tutors and tutees. The world around them becomes the basis of their learning, of the new words they learn, of the new words they write. Instead of discovering words in a workbook conceived by someone else, they discover them in their own neighborhoods, in their own lives, and in their own families. The child himself, his neighbors, and his family become the content of the curriculum.

Much of the YTY training attempts to help free the tutor of preconceived notions of what teaching and learning are all about. There is no notion of making the tutor a reading specialist or having him compete with professionals. Rather the program asks the tutor and tutee to develop a relationship, to develop new kinds of learning about who they are and how they connect with the world. YTY believes that as they develop more positive feelings about themselves, the more confident they will be in whatever instruction they "receive" in the regular school. The tutors with improved self-definition begin to see themselves differently and to see what potential they have. This change may result in a change of attitude toward learning in school.

The basic belief of YTY is that there is tremendous learning power in the tutor that needs to be unleashed. Only through being given clear responsibility and opportunity to use his own initiative will the underachieving tutor realize this potential. Thus, while the program provides considerable support and training for the tutor, he is given an enormous range of freedom to foster his self-development. The training program emphasizes this self-development, self-discovery, and opportunity to explore rather than highly specific programmed tutoring techniques. So, for example, the tutors are encouraged to develop their own tutoring techniques, ideas, and games, and the tutors put out their own newsletter. It is felt that tutor-made materials are more effective than commercial materials, which should only be used to supplement original ones.

Many of the tutors spend hours of their leisure time in creating games to teach reading to their tutees. A few examples extracted from several hundred follow:

A sturdy *paper tree*, its branches hung with word cards spelling out the things seen during a walk in the park (a "bug," a "fish"). New word cards are substituted as the vocabulary builds.

Flash cards, made of colored construction paper, illustrated with lively pictures and words or letters of the alphabet.

An *alphabet game* with a bingo format, used to give practice in matching upper- and lower-case letters.

A *wheel game*, which exposes a series of pictures, one at a time, and a clock hand with which children can point to the first letter of the object pictured (television set, watch, car).

Picture analysis books, made from magazine pictures. One tutor wrote a brief description of how the books were used:

> Picture Analysis is a game of thought where a person holds a picture with no writing in front of another person and that person is supposed to tell what the picture is saying.

Crossword puzzles, containing from simple to complex combinations of words.

A *pinball word-building game* for the teaching of grammar, made from cardboard boxes and containing all the ingredients of the usual pinball machine.

YTY is not a remedial program, although there is some remedial work done under the supervision of trained personnel; the main emphasis is on *learning to learn through learning to teach*.

A related goal of the program is to humanize learning. In this sense YTY is part of the overall trend reflected in the British infant schools, in the "street academy" approach of the Urban League, and in the "free schools" and other approaches developing around the world. These approaches are directed toward making learning less stiff, more down to earth, more funlike, free, and open ended, emphasizing discovery and self-development, utilizing the style of the learner rather than imposing some standard school style or curriculum. Thus the YTY January 31, 1969, report states:

> Youth Tutoring Programs should not have a classroom atmosphere nor should they have a playground atmosphere. When asked to advise the program, some reading experts have tended to inhibit tutors, imposing traditional rigid standards upon them. They have understood mistakenly that YTY is

merely an extension of regular school work. Other people have damaged the program by viewing it in the opposite extreme. YTY is a place for play involving older and younger kids, they seem to think. Neither of the above cases represents a program that benefits youth. Somewhere in between the two extremes lies YTY, a program that combines personal responsibility and creativity with the seriousness of real work.

Observation of the tutoring sessions reveals what seems to be little difference between work and play because it all looks like fun. The most striking difference between the YTY session and school is the obvious relationship of affection and respect that is built up between the tutor and the tutee. One sees this relationship in their physical closeness, in their walking with arms around each other, and in the worship in the eyes of the tutee watching every change of expression of his tutor. Another obvious difference is in the number of activities going on at the same time; when one teacher is conducting a class of thirty children, it is much easier to have all children working on the same type of activity at the same time. Since each tutoring pair in YTY works independently from one another, it is not unusual to see each pair working on a completely different activity. Because the tutors develop their own lesson plans and create their own materials, an observer is apt to see a much greater variety of learning materials in a YTY center than in a traditional classroom; the tutors try not to rely on the classroom textbooks the tutee has been using during the regular school day.

Most visitors to YTY centers find the informal atmosphere quite different from the atmosphere in a classroom; if the tutor and tutee find it easier to work on the floor, they sit on the floor. The tutors and tutees both might call the adult supervisor by his first name, even though he is a classroom teacher and is called Mr. —— during the school day. The tutors and tutees feel free to call across the room to another

pair to "come see what we're doing." Perhaps the most re-
vealing difference between a YTY center and a traditional
classroom is that very often a visitor to a YTY center has
difficulty in spotting the supervisor immediately. In most
traditional classrooms a visitor can spot the teacher at once
by looking toward the front of the room or by looking in
the direction that the children are. The YTY supervisor works
in the background of the program as supportive personnel,
and the attention of the tutors and tutees is focused on each
other, not on the supervisor.

Early in the development of the YTY program a serious
handicap developed when remedial reading specialists were
introduced as trainers of the tutors. The reading specialists
brought expertise, which they tried to pass on to the tutors;
the tutors settled back into their previous behavioral attitude,
rejecting "school as usual." A few tried to substitute this
method of tutoring for the more creative approach that had
been their pattern. It was a catastrophe for both groups. *The
remedial reading teachers did not succeed in making the tutors
into miniature reading experts,* and the tutors lost interest in
tutoring and closed their minds to this type of didactic instruction. The specialists did not seem aware of the tutors'
ability to establish rapport in the one-to-one relationship, nor
were they responsive to the flexibility and creativity with
which the tutors had turned a wide variety of informal behaviors and experiences into occasions for developing language skills. For example, the tutors prepared and organized
the tutees to interview people on the street, accompanying
the tutees while they did so, then discussing what happened
and inspiring the tutees to write about the experience. *The
reading teachers saw this as "fun," not "learning"!*

The work of the reading specialists was curtailed and
leaders were obtained for the weekly in-service training session
who were more sensitive to the potential of the tutors and

the need for fostering the relationship between tutor and tutee. As it developed, the reading specialists became a resource to whom the tutors turned for advice as it was needed and the youngsters settled into the type of tutoring they had used earlier. However, from this experience the Commission learned how very important it is to have all facets of a school system in complete understanding of the goals of the program and of the methods that can best achieve those goals.

MORE THAN READING SCORES

We indicated in Chapter II that there has been significant improvement in the reading achievement of the YTY tutors. But equally important are the attitudinal and behavioral effects.

Punctuality has become the accepted norm of the program where the tutor sees himself as responsible for his tutee. Some teachers have commented that after the tutor has been in the program for a while he begins to show more interest in his own classwork; for instance, he might develop enough self-confidence to raise his hand in answer to a teacher's question; he might begin to be prepared for his own classes, rather than forgetting his books or pen; he might start telling the teacher about his tutoring.

The tutor's interest can be judged by the long hours he puts into his work at night in preparation for his next day; in the fact that the tutor spends *his own money in taking the tutee to a movie;* in the fact that parents seek help from the tutors when the program ends by suggesting that they, the parents, pay a small amount for continued tutoring. The behavior of disruptive tutors changes drastically when they have charge of their own tutees. In Philadelphia, for example, despite the fact that the tutors were previously alienated from school and had serious "behavior problems," not one of them had to be removed from the project because of misconduct.

The following typical letters from tutors to the parents of tutees give some indication of what has been happening to the tutors themselves:

8–21–70

To the Parents of Jimmy:

I have worked with Jimmy over the summer working mostly in math and reading. Jimmy has a poor math average. But I think it has improved from the test and drills I gave him. His reading has improved in the way that he now trys. At the beginning of the summer, if he didn't know a word he would stop and wouldn't try, now he trys and usually gets it right. Although it is hard to keep Jimmy interested he is a nice boy to work with.

Sincerely, Charlene
Tutor

7–22–69

To the Parents of Bryon:

Unfortunately not very much in the way of school work was accomplished with Bryon during the program due to his unwillingness to work. I think Bryon's main problem for not cooperating is his fear of failing. He can do good work and will do good work until he gets corrected, from then on his work begins to downgrade, and at times Bryon completely refuses to go on. Under these conditions it was very hard to get much done considering the fact that corrections had to be given in order for Bryon to improve. The one thing that I found which could get Bryon to work was to praise him when he did good work thus encouraging him to continue, and saving the corrections till the end. As far as trips and other activities were concerned, Bryon was very cooperative. Prob-

81

ably because he wasn't being forced to go, but rather due to the fact that he wanted to. I believe that once Bryon is able to accept corrections without getting discouraged tremendous progress will be made.

Sincerely, William
Tutor

FROM DEMONSTRATION TO IMPLEMENTATION

The YTY program originally developed as a demonstration program in two cities—Philadelphia and Newark in the summer of 1967 and the first part of 1968. From these early demonstration projects the Commission then set out to achieve the implementation phase of the project, "to teach educators, school administrators, teachers, and local Neighborhood Youth Corps officials the need, value and *modus operandi* of the Youth Tutoring Youth program in a large number of cities."

The demonstration phase of the Youth Tutoring Youth program resulted in a model that could be implemented elsewhere. The following is the model's strategy for implementation. The Commission first brings the efficacy of the program to the attention of a member of the Board of Education or to the superintendent of a school system. When it receives a commitment from the superintendent that the program will be implemented in his system, the Commission invites to a workshop three of the school personnel. Usually the three people who attend the workshop are (1) an associate or assistant superintendent, (2) a person who will head the local YTY program, and (3) the administrator in charge of the program from which the tutors and supervisor will be drawn, such as the Neighborhood Youth Corps director or dropout prevention director.

The purpose of the workshops is to "show and teach"

educators the value of a Youth Tutoring Youth program and how to institute it. The workshops are planned around preparing the interns either to run an In-School Neighborhood Youth Corps Tutoring Program or to be able to tell someone else how to do it. The interns' days, often twelve hours or more, are packed with activity. The premise is that the participants will learn how to operate a tutoring project and will be convinced of the merits of doing so by immersing themselves, through active involvement with staff and tutors, in an ongoing program.

The workshops run from two to six days; they always take place in cities where there is an ongoing YTY program so that the interns can observe and work in the tutoring centers. The interns begin to see that the tutees can be helped by tutors who are underachievers from the same background as the tutees. The interns, who see the tutors taking responsibility and becoming involved in how to learn as they teach younger children, are usually a bit surprised at the seriousness of purpose the teen-age tutors show and at their creativity, as seen in the learning materials, games, and booklets they develop. They are impressed with the way the young people greet each other and how they work. The tutor and tutee might dramatize a story they are reading; they might act it out; they might go for a walk in the playground or they may be deeply involved in reading a book they had previously written. Often the tutor acts as the private secretary for his tutee as the little one dictates his story or a play that he wants to put on for the other tutees. The interns note the way the tutors almost always gravitate to giving direction by questions, not immediately telling the tutee an unknown word but asking such questions as "What does a bunny do?"

Besides learning about the program by working with the tutors, *the interns also learn how to organize and set up a program and how to secure funds for its operation.* The notion that a center supervisor can be an older teen-ager as well as a teacher seems to surprise the participants. Generally it is arranged that the trainees visit centers run by each of the three types of supervisors used in the programs—paraprofessionals, older teen-agers, and professional teachers. They observe how each supervisor brings a special advantage: teachers bring instructional experience, paraprofessionals bring an understanding of the neighborhood from which they came and a ready acceptance of the underachieving tutor as a person with real potential, and the older teen-ager brings a rapport that only youth can establish with each other. The centers operated by teen-age supervisors usually attract the most attention.

Many of the techniques used in the interns' training were suggested by Gerald Weinstein[1] of the University of Massachusetts. The purpose of this aspect of the training is to give the interns some feeling for the kind of training that is later to be passed on in the development of the tutors. The making out of scraps of paper, ribbon, material, and other odd items a collage of oneself, for example, is a way of getting through the constraints on communication that have been built into our civilized, polite society. The interns reveal themselves more readily through this means than through formal, uptight, conventional conversation. After making the collages, interns pair up and, less shy of expressing themselves, share feelings. This method often brings out heretofore hidden uniqueness in each individual.

Almost all the training is concentrated in the affective domain. The aim is to get the interns to "hang loose" about what the tutors will be doing, and to create an atmosphere in which the tutors can be freed of their usual concept of school,

---

1. Gerald Weinstein and Mario D. Fantini, *Toward Humanistic Education, A Curriculum of Affect* (New York: Praeger Publications, 1970; published for the Ford Foundation).

enabling them to establish rapport in their own way with their tutees and to invent their own approaches to learning.

Since the inception of the first Youth Tutoring Youth program, the Commission has conducted 34 workshops, which trained 1,460 persons from 388 school systems and 224 community action agencies.

LINKAGES

Youth Tutoring Youth is a natural component for many existing educational programs, and the most successful YTY programs are those which have linked into these other programs. The most common linkage is with Title I of the Elementary and Secondary Education Act (ESEA). Title I funds can be used to pay supervisors, purchase supplies, provide snacks, and even to pay tutors. The federal programs coordinators of many school systems have said that YTY is an ideal program for Title I, since both the tutor and the tutee benefit from the program, not just the tutee; they feel that service is being provided two students for the price of one.

The Career Opportunities Program, funded under the Bureau of Educational Personnel Development of the U.S. Office of Education, has included YTY as the first step on the ladder to a career in education. Currently there are more than 130 of these programs funded throughout the United States. In some of the COP projects, the tutors are guaranteed employment by the school system as classroom aides when they have completed high school. When serving as aides they attend a local college or university—tuition and books paid for by COP—and at the end of four years they can be certified as classroom teachers. A few of the COP projects offer the tutors *practicum* credit for their work; these credits are held in escrow by the college until the tutors graduate from high school. Once they begin their college courses toward certification, these credits count toward their degree. For many of the tutors, participation in a COP project is their only means of attending college.

The Office of Economic Opportunity has encouraged local community action agencies to participate in YTY programs; as a result, in some cities these agencies are working with school systems to provide such necessities as supervision, space, and transportation for field trips. VISTA workers have started YTY programs in remote areas where no other federal programs are operating.

In the spring of 1970 the Office of Economic Opportunity, the U.S. Office of Education, and the U.S. Department of Labor issued a joint intention of supporting the President's Right to Read campaign through Youth Tutoring Youth programs all over the country. As a result of this concentration of effort, the number of YTY programs tripled; programs were started in cities where one local agency working by itself could not fund all the necessary parts of the program, but three agencies (i.e., the Neighborhood Youth Corps, the community action agency, and the school system) could pool their resources and start one program, sponsored by all three agencies.

Sources of funding for various components of a Youth Tutoring Youth program are many: some of the most commonly used are Titles I, III, VII, and VIII of the Elementary and Secondary Education Act; Model Cities; Education Professions Development Act; school budget funds; VISTA; other OEO funds; Teacher Corps; and college work-study programs. Such organizations as 4-H Clubs, Campfire Girls, Boy and Girl Scouts are also linked to some of the YTY programs. The YTY program that is supported by many sources of funding will survive; the program that depends on one source of funding may be doomed if that source gives out.

YTY believes that the successful implementation of its program is based upon five fundamental principles: (1) a carefully developed internship program (and refresher workshops) for administrators, supervisors, and other personnel; (2) the development of materials for use by the supervisors and administrators; (3) the winning of a solid commitment of the administrators to the program; (4) the careful assignment of a specific person who will have as his sole responsibility the carrying out of the program at the local level; (5) the encouragement of flexible modification of the YTY design to make it applicable to specific local conditions.

VARIATIONS ON THE YTY THEME

While operating within the broad framework of program design developed by the NCRY,[2] the YTY programs in the various cities develop a character of their own.

In Trinidad, Colorado, the program is operated almost completely by tutors. There is an administrator, but the elected officers among the tutors handle all the correspondence, the gathering of materials, and all the mechanical items usually assigned to an administrator; they contact the press, and they help recruit the tutees.

In the original St. Louis, Missouri, program the tutors were

2. A panoply of manuals, guides, pamphlets, films, film clips, and other such aids have been developed by the National Commission. These include, in addition to reports on various project grants cited previously, "A Manual for Trainers," a "Supervisor's Manual," pamphlets for tutors, "You're the Tutor," and a periodic newsletter of the same name, also resource booklets for tutors entitled "For the Tutor," "Tutoring Tricks and Treats." These are available from the National Commission for Resources for Youth, 36 West 44 Street, N.Y., N.Y., 10036.

underachieving junior high school students who returned to their former elementary schools to tutor younger children. Since there was no money for supervision, the seven or eight tutors in each of the elementary schools tutored in rooms fairly near the offices of the principals, who were willing to oversee the program. They managed the tutoring every day without a supervisor, and the part-time administrator led the in-service training session once a week. Placing these under-achieving tutors in the school they formerly attended did much to reinforce them. Their former teachers stopped by to utter such words of encouragement as "You're doing a good job." Teachers who remembered these tutors as discipline problems saw them in a different light.

In New Haven, Connecticut, the Black Educators Organization, a coalition of teachers concerned with working with inner-city children, took the local leadership, obtained foundation funds to support the YTY program, and trained community persons to serve as tutor supervisors.

In Florence, Alabama, the program was initiated for the first time in the summer of 1969. During the eight-week session, tutor attendance was 100 percent, and an average of 1.1 year gains were achieved by tutors, based upon the Diagnostic Reading Tests.

In Washington, D.C., the program began in the summer of 1968. Operating in groups of fifteen tutors, there were seven centers serving four hundred tutees. Both tutors and tutees attended Title I (ESEA) schools and were two or more years behind in reading. Paraprofessionals, some of whom had formerly been tutors, have come to play a key role in the local centers. During the school day the aides serve as liaison between school and home, and after school hours they supervise the centers.

In Phoenix, Arizona, the first program began in the summer of 1970. Twenty-six eighth-graders tutored forty younger children, first- through fourth-graders; both groups were a year or more behind in reading. Tutor gains for the eight weeks averaged 1.83 grades, with some gains as high as 5.0 grades. The Phoenix program is cautious about these dramatic increases. "It is obvious from the dramatic increases in reading that tutors could not have *learned* up to five grade levels in eight weeks. Rather, it is apparent that most of these children had a potential reading level higher than their school performances indicated. These potentials were brought out and augmented in the Youth Tutoring Youth program because the tutors were given respect, confidence, and relevant reading materials."[3]

In the Los Angeles, California, City Schools, the Crenshaw Community Youth Study Association has sponsored, for the past four years, a Youth Tutoring Youth program which has been used to teach a particular method of reading—"formula phonics"—which appears to have special efficacy for Mexican-American students. Prior to the use of underachieving tutors, only professional teachers were considered adequate to use this method, but when underachieving youth were used as part of a team of five, it was found that youthful tutors had as beneficial an effect on tutees as did professional teachers.

In Miami, Florida, the Youth Tutoring Youth Program of the public schools has been linked with the J. F. Kennedy Awards Program of the Miami-Dade Junior College. The tutors are Neighborhood Youth Corps enrollees who are supervised by the JFK Awards Program junior college students, who are supervised in turn by graduate students and, of course, by the director of the program.

In Two Villages, New Mexico, young tutors are used in a unique way. Since Pueblo is not a written language, and since the young do not learn crafts, it is not likely that the tribe's

3. Lucy Bartholomew and Heather Gurley, " 'Youth Tutoring Youth' in South Phoenix: Results and Accomplishments" (August 20, 1970), p. 2.

crafts will be transmitted to other generations. Therefore, a plan has been devised whereby teen-age tutors teach a craft (and learn it while doing so) to younger children. This has proved very successful both for the tutor and the tutee. Pictures and slides of the children are sent to adjoining villages, to encourage other Pueblo groups to develop similar "tutoring" programs.

In Lewiston, Maine, some of the high school tutors themselves are responsible for the organization of the program. For instance, three such tutors attended an NCRY workshop to learn training techniques, and they in turn will train other tutors.

In Fall River, Massachusetts, YTY is a component of the Title VIII ESEA Drop-Out Prevention Program. In an attempt to get the tutors involved in administrative decision-making, they also serve on an advisory council made up of students, teachers, and aides; there is a parent advisory council that functions with it. Another Title VIII program in Baltimore also has a YTY component. A team of their school-year tutors were hired during the summer to evaluate the previous year's program and to plan materials and training for the new school-year program. This team will help to train the new tutors, and will serve as consultants as well as tutors.

In Boston, Massachusetts, there are a wide variety of tutoring programs. In one school, tutoring is used in a deliberate attempt to ease racial tension. This school jumped from 55 percent white and 45 percent black to 90 percent black and 10 percent Puerto Rican within a three-year period; the emphasis in this tutoring program, therefore, is on setting up a climate in which the blacks and the Puerto Ricans can get to know and understand one another. For instance, the blacks tutor the Puerto Ricans in English and the Puerto Ricans tutor the blacks in street Spanish.

At one time in Cleveland, Ohio, fatherless boys were used

as tutors in order that they might form a relationship with younger boys who were also fatherless. This project was designed as an after-school program in a particular school where there were a large number of ADC parents; using foundation funds, the program concentrated on trying to build a good male relationship between the two groups of boys.

In San Diego, California, the school system developed its YTY program as a means for students and community personnel to participate in an educational program that is part of a career ladder, the goal of which is ultimately to prepare them for careers in teaching and related fields. Tutors in San Diego get a real taste of teaching and classroom mechanics. They go into the elementary school classrooms during the day to assist the teachers. Under the teacher's direction, a tutor may work with a small group of children in such activities as reading and writing, or he may take one child aside to help him with a specific problem. The tutor does not always work with the same child, but always in the same classroom, where he is familiar and popular with the children. The children see him as a model of responsibility and leadership. When school ends, and most children and teachers leave, the tutor, an NYC enrollee, meets with his own tutee in a classroom.

In Chicago, Illinois, some of the supervisors are older Neighborhood Youth Corps enrollees. Staff takes the better students and involves them in the development of the program, and from this group evolve the leaders who act as supervisors. Almost all of these are former tutors with the program, and some of them are junior college students who come back to serve as supervisors in the summer. They are all from the same neighborhood as the tutees.

In Chinle, Arizona, at Rough Rock Demonstration School on the Navajo Indian Reservation, the older children teach English to the younger children who speak only Navajo.

Besides the YTY design there are many variations of tutoring programs that might meet specific needs. In Portland, Oregon, a large tutorial program has been in operation for several years in which high school youngsters receive credit for tutoring elementary school children. Early in the program transportation was a problem, but the program managed to secure volunteer help from a nearby community center; a bus and private cars were made available to take the tutors from the high schools to the elementary schools. Someone in the superintendent's office has now been assigned to help develop more tutorial programs throughout the school system. At the Jefferson High School there is a tutorial center in operation for every period of the day, with high school students tutoring others who need extra help in math and English.

In Ocean Hill–Brownsville, New York, during the demonstration period in P.S. 144, a tutoring program was carried on using fifth-graders to teach second-graders. For one period, for four days per week, fifth-graders went to the second-grade classroom. On the fifth day they met together in their own classroom to receive instruction in how to tutor and for feedback as to what had happened in their tutoring sessions. These were "disruptive" children not considered academically superior, and yet they made tremendous gains and overcame their deficits. They frankly confessed that before they were tutors their game was to bug the teacher in "try to get me" and other antics, but that once they were given an opportunity to accept the responsibility, they had settled down to the serious business of tutoring.

In the Germantown Area Schools Program, Philadelphia, Pennsylvania, there is a "do-in," in which older students aid second-graders with reading and community understanding through walking tours of the neighborhood. The older children help the younger ones to describe and interpret what they see in the neighborhood through pictures (photographs and drawings) and stories and improvisational drama (role playing, with puppets representing family and community figures).

Student-produced stories, photographs, and drawings resulting from the tours have been collected into an urban primer—*What Do We Need in Our Neighborhood?*—used in the Philadelphia public schools.

In Project Clinic, San Miguel School, Sunnyvale, California, seventh- and eighth-grade underachievers tutor in the very skill in which they are deficient. The rationale for the use of this form of tutoring is the assumption that the tutor will react in the following fashion: "I'm not so good at this skill, but the teacher seems confident that I can learn it and she even thinks I can learn it well enough to teach it to someone else. If I'm going to teach it, I'd better learn it extra well."

In Central High School and Roosevelt Elementary School, Detroit, Michigan, high school students receive academic credit for helping younger children with their schoolwork. The older students are part of a general introductory psychology class.

In the cross-age tutoring program, a part of Community Action Against Poverty, Inc., Muskegan, Michigan, an outstanding feature is the orientation given to tutors at the beginning of the program. Orientation is provided by members of the black community and members of the staff of the anti-poverty agency to make the tutors more responsive to the needs and expectations of the youngsters, the school, and the community.

In South High School, Salt Lake City, Utah, teen-agers worked with emotionally disturbed elementary school youngsters during regular school time. Twice a month they met with a high school counselor, the teacher of the emotionally disturbed, and a Board of Education social worker to discuss their work with the children and their feelings about the experience.

SOME ESSENTIAL INGREDIENTS FOR A SUCCESSFUL PROGRAM

In each of the 250 school systems now operating YTY, there is such a variety of techniques and approaches that one cannot say that there is one YTY model. However, to have a successful program the Commission feels that the following are essential ingredients:

1. *A climate of acceptance.* It is essential that YTY be inaugurated in a school system where there is a climate of acceptance. As the program is established in the schools, it is important to convince the principal, the parents, and the teachers regarding what YTY is intended to do. A principal or a janitor can block the program very readily; they must be sold on it before it is started in the school. The parents should be brought into the program from the outset, not only through attendance at large meetings but by meeting and talking with tutors. They should be encouraged to drop in on the program whenever possible.

2. *Administration.* The program should have an administrator. The original programs chose professional educators as administrators; while this is desirable it is not essential. Some of the newer programs have successfully used people from outside the school system as administrators.

The supervisors can be professional teachers, paraprofessionals, persons from the community, or college students. They should be assigned on the basis of one supervisor for every fifteen to twenty tutors, depending on the capacity of the supervisor. NCRY prefers paraprofessional supervisors. The paraprofessional from the neighborhood usually doesn't expect trouble from the youngster, and generally doesn't get it.

Much of the success of the tutors depends on the supervisor's confidence that the children can learn by informal methods. The paraprofessional seems ready to concentrate on the assets of the youngsters and to minimize their liabilities.

3. *Space.* The principal must designate some space for use by the tutors. Sometimes the tutoring sessions are given four or five classrooms not in use after school, where four to six pairs of tutor-tutees conduct their sessions. Other times they are assigned to the library, the cafeteria, the infirmary, or even to the hall. Tutoring can take place in a wide variety of settings, but there should be some place that the tutor can call his own and that gives him privacy for the time he is with his tutee. Furthermore, it is important that there be a place where tutors can lock up their materials at the end of a school day. Materials left in a classroom become a source of irritation to the regular classroom teacher. Tutoring should be provided in the elementary school, if possible, since liaison with the teachers of the tutees will be readily available and thus the teachers will have an opportunity to observe the tutors' sessions.

4. *Tutoring sessions.* The sessions should last from an hour and a half to two hours each day. For the most part, the tutoring sessions in YTY are built around the teaching of reading, since both tutors and tutees need this desperately. The crux of the sessions, however, is individual instruction. With few exceptions each tutor has one or at the most two tutees, and he deals with them as individuals.

While the tutors map out daily lesson plans and keep a log of the day's lessons, they should always be flexible. A well-organized lesson plan might have to be abandoned because of the state of mind of a tutee on a particular day. "My tutee is tired today and doesn't want to read." Tutors must accommodate themselves to the loosening up of feelings. If they discover a deficiency in their tutees' learning they must quickly invent methods of meeting it. For instance, a boy whose tutee would never apply himself, whose mind was wandering around the room and never seemed to get to a book or to his writing—began by having his tutee make a map of the room. This idea grew, and each day the tutee would be called upon to make a map of another part of the school or of his home. The tutee never knew when he would be called on to deliver another map, so he formed the habit of observing what was going on around him; by this method the tutor was able to bring his attention to the lesson at hand.

5. *Materials.* Securing materials for the tutee is no problem —a few pencils, some paper, crayons, magazines, and scissors are about all that is needed, and often the tutors bring these from their homes. They even make much of the reading material by having the tutees dictate stories, plays, and other works to them. However, the tutors should also have access to a wide variety of reading materials from the beginning reader on, including paperbacks for those who become capable of ready reading. A supply of books is often hard for the tutors to come by. Many times they are not in the elementary schools where the tutoring sessions take place, and arrangements have to be made for them to be readily accessible, possibly on loan from the library.

While the Commission's main concern has been with the rapid spread of the YTY program to after-school programs throughout the country, it has also helped develop spin-offs into the school system itself. A well-run YTY program presents a convincing model of how school could be different. *In YTY there is no tracking, no negative self-fulfilling prophecy, because everyone is expected to learn.*

There is increasing evidence that the program is spreading within the school system during the school day. This is reflected in the great variety of programs we have referred to throughout in which there is increased recognition that youngsters can learn through teaching, that learning is more than a programmed, formal, teacher-to-child type of operation. Of course, it is difficult to judge how much YTY has directly influenced this trend, because there are many other programs following the LTT model and the whole "informal" education trend is undoubtedly having its own influence. YTY converges with, reinforces, and is reinforced by this larger trend, while always recognizing that *learning through teaching consists of much more than the informalizing of education.*

CHAPTER V

No directive from Washington, no dramatic book, no authoritative bit of research prompted the increasing number of school programs in which students today are teaching each other. Rather, these tutoring experiments have risen spontaneously and simultaneously in many parts of the country, and have taken a great number of different forms.[1]

How to Do It

The review of programs involving children teaching other children in Chapters II and IV confirms the variety suggested by Thelen. The range is from after-school to in-school programs, from use of peers as teachers to cross-age efforts, and from programs in which learning through teaching is an adjunct to other activities to those where it is the central feature of the school. It would be foolhardy to suggest—no less prescribe—any single way to design a learning through teaching project. Rather, we will suggest the various dimensions that should be considered, describe pertinent experiences, and suggest various possible designs. Indeed, as we indicated in Chapter IV, the largest such program, the Youth Tutoring

1. Herbert A. Thelen, "Tutoring by Students . . . ," p. 229.

Youth effort, itself emphasizes the need for local flexibility within the broad program framework.

The components of programs of children teaching other children include administration, the children, the adult teachers and other staff, logistics of space and materials, and evaluation.

ADMINISTRATION

Central to any program is the *commitment* of agency leaders. Since learning through teaching programs challenge many present school practices, and since there is danger that they may be diluted into mere tutoring programs, understanding must be clear and commitment knowledgeably given. While practices will vary depending upon the particular design, especially whether the program is to be a part of the formal school activities or an adjunct to them, it would be well for both the school board and the chief executive officer to be familiar with the program intent and design. Perhaps the most important notion is that of accepting a design that sees sources of learning other than the teacher alone.

As indicated in Chapter IV, the National Commission on Resources for Youth seeks to achieve this initial awareness through bringing to their training sessions three persons: an administrator at the superintendent level, a person representing the local funding source,[2] and the person who will actually operate the Youth Tutoring Youth program. Two-to five-day training sessions allow time both for the National Commission to present its material and point of view and for the local people to begin to thrash out actual implementation

2. The tutors in the National Commission on Resources for Youth's programs are usually recruited from and paid by the Neighborhood Youth Corps.

issues. Of course, differing sponsorship or administration arrangements will suggest other configurations of participation than the trio attending the National Commission's sessions. However, what may be generally useful is the seeking of informal discussion of the program, setting aside special time for consideration of it, involving at the outset several people from different perspectives.

While local practices of implementation will vary, equally important is involvement of all levels of the institutional hierarchy—district superintendents, building principals, and individual teachers. Assuming that the program is meant to be more than simply a nice addition to regular activities, the process of informing and involving all of the relevant players at an early stage is crucial.

The process of initial orientation should immediately include lay leadership—school board, community boards, and both parent groups and individual parents of participating children. The learning through teaching program incorporates several features that will need clarification. Perhaps from the parents' perspective, the two basic issues can be put thusly: "How will my child learn if he is taught by another child rather than a teacher?" and "Why should I send my child to school to do the teacher's work of teaching instead of being taught?" There are, of course, real answers to these questions—answers this book, at least in part, seeks to present, answers that have been given to parents in communities where programs now operate, and accepted by them as satisfactory. Essentially the answers have to do with the positive gains for the children involved. But these and similar questions must be sought out and answered, not only before the program begins but as part of an ongoing process.

The role of administration carries beyond the stage of program introduction to that of operation. Regardless of the setting, essential to the effectiveness of the program is that a *single individual have central and clear responsibility for the program.* This may vary from the administrator in a Neighborhood Youth Corps-sponsored Youth Tutoring Youth program, to a building supervisor if the program operates in one school, to a system-wide member of the superintendent's staff. While essentially a simple notion, the management of programs involving children teaching other children is sufficiently complex—not to say anything of its importance—to demand such attention.

Where the program is part of the school day and thus includes the active involvement of the regular adult teachers, the administrative staff's role is one of scheduling, managing, consulting, and at least organizing training. Key roles must be established for the teachers of both the children teaching and those being taught. Where the program is after school and essentially adjunctive to the regular school program, the administrator takes on additional roles, including liaison with the children's regular teachers,[3] as well as supervising each of the centers.

The National Commission on Resources for Youth has had considerable success in using paraprofessionals as directors of its tutoring centers. In Washington, D.C., for example, younger Neighborhood Youth Corps members tutor, older ones supervise and train tutors, and paraprofessionals are in charge of the tutoring centers. This model of involving both youngsters and paraprofessionals in key roles could well be carried over to those programs operating within the regular school structure.[4]

More than any factor other than the power of the learning through teaching mechanism itself, management will deter-

3. We will discuss this role more fully below in the sections on the children, the adults, and training.
4. The incorporation of Youth Tutoring Youth programs in the new Career Opportunities Program is likely to produce further developments in community tutoring programs involving paraprofessionals.

mine the success of the program. The process of most school bureaucracies, unfortunately, works against the success of programs such as those discussed here. *Too often there is a diffusion of effort, a failure to set priorities, a top-down, noninvolving pattern of leadership.* Also, a program such as learning through teaching, with its potentially broad ramifications, may be seen as a way to "solve" too many other school problems.

Program managers need to consider the history and special experiences of the particular school and system within which they operate in order to understand the impact this new program will make. The problems of operating within the school setting lead many to consider operating programs outside of the school day and outside of the regular school context. Such a decision, of course, is a matter to be determined in the light of local conditions, balancing the likelihood of greater freedom and less bureaucracy outside of the school with the possibility of greater support and more direct effect and opportunity for change within the school. In any case, *a climate of support* must be developed. The Pocoima and Yonkers programs have made special efforts to involve, along with teachers and students, parents and the larger community. Some programs may have neither the desire nor resources to undertake the elaborate sequence of sensitivity sessions, teacher and parent workshops, and other features that have been used at Pocoima. What is necessary, however, is the conscious effort to gain understanding and to build support as an ongoing feature of the program.

The management and administrative problem can perhaps be summarized by saying that while there may be *several* ways to succeed there are *many* ways to fail.

THE CHILDREN: TEACHERS AND PUPILS

Selection

The first issue, of course, is whether the program will be for an entire group of children—a whole grade, school, district, or system—or only for certain selected children. A powerful point is that by placing a child in the tutor role without setting arbitrary standards, one is placing him "in a position of trust and responsibility, thereby invoking change in behavior rather than having evidence of change be a prerequisite to be given responsibility."[5] This notion is akin to what may be the key lesson of the federal antipoverty program, that *opportunity itself produces motivation* rather than the old notion of not offering opportunity until proper motivation is displayed.

If all members of a particular group are to participate either in the teaching or pupil role, or both, there is no issue of selection. If, however, only a portion of the children are to participate, there must be established a basis for inclusion.

Those programs which include only a portion of the children have always done so on a voluntary basis. In the Youth Tutoring Youth program the tutors have come from among youngsters eligible for Neighborhood Youth Corps programs who have not been doing well in school. And, as the National Commission's Lorraine Kavanagh puts it, "The only difference between the tutor and tutee is age. Otherwise, they both come from the same neighborhoods, and essentially the same

5. "Benefits Reported by Users of Cross-Age Helping Programs" (Center for Research on Utilization of Scientific Knowledge, University of Michigan, n.d.), p. 2.

backgrounds." The experience of the teachers in a North Carolina Youth Tutoring Youth program may be typical.

> In the beginning the professional staff was concerned over the selection of tutors. They were in total agreement that tutors should be Juniors or Seniors with a high academic standing. Experience has changed our minds about this. The emphasis now is on characteristics such as dependability, trustworthiness, a cooperative attitude and a concern for children. In many cases, the professional staff feels that the less academically talented tutor can empathize better with the tutee experiencing difficulty.[6]

Other programs have not been as insistent as the National Commission that the tutors be themselves poor students. However, one must avoid the potential stigmatization of the program being one of "smart" kids tutoring "dumb" ones or only dumb kids in the program. Therefore, it may seem useful to recruit youngsters across the full range of ability as both tutors and tutees, if not concentrating on underachieving ones who can be especially benefited and, perhaps, make a special contribution, as the following example suggests.

> Richard had come recommended to YTY as a boy who needed special help and who was below average on the California Mental Maturity Test (as were most of our tutors). Richard immediately revealed a capacity for leadership. He encouraged all of the tutors to work hard and he voiced concern about the personal problems of his tutee. One of the tutors wrote, "I like Richard, he doesn't play around and he can be funny and he has a good head and pays off his debts too." Richard was the most dependable youngster in the program, besides being the

---

6. Darrell Spencer, "Neighborhood Youth Corps Tutorial Program" (Raleigh, North Carolina, Public Schools, Summer 1970), p. 1.

most creative. He had enough self-direction to begin with so the YTY program enhanced his abilities.[7]

At the Custer School, Monroe, Michigan, the principal selected ten of the most disruptive fifth-graders as tutors. "He wanted to help them change their self-image from 'bad' guys to one of 'good' guys who are helping the system."[8] While not recommended as a selection criterion, it is interesting that at Pocoima

> some of the first tutors selected were "social-adjustment students"—students who had been problems in their own classes— but kindergarten teachers were not aware of this and were amazed when they found out. These students performed so well and maturely as tutors, and related so well to the kindergarten children, that it was hard to imagine them as problem children.[9]

The cross-age program makes the interesting point that if one mixes both the high-peer-status children with the less successful, "it gives the hitherto unsuccessful olders a chance to work with successful classmates of high peer status, thus broadening their range of possible friendships and perceived influence."[10]

A number of programs have had success in using the entire older class as tutors. In those instances in which a particular child did not seem able to work with the smaller children, another role in the program was assigned (e.g., posting schedules, making materials).[11] To be sure, *not all children*

7. Lucy Bartholomew and Heather Gurley, "'Youth Tutoring Youth' in South Phoenix . . . ," p. 6.
8. Lippitt, Eiseman, and Lippitt, *Cross-Age Helping Program* . . . , p. 51.
9. Newmark and Melaragno, "Tutorial Community Project: Report . . . ," p. 26.
10. Lippitt, Eiseman, and Lippitt, *Cross-Age Helping Program* . . . , p. 51.
11. Newmark and Melaragno, "Tutorial Community Project: Report . . . ," p. 16.

like to tutor. "Some children could not persevere in patiently assisting the slow student; others could not see that learning is not an automatic 'teacher teaches—student learns' situation; a few encountered students who were difficult to control because of emotional or psychological problems."[12]

A quite different approach was used at University City, Missouri.[13] In order to be selected the junior high school students had to learn and demonstrate proficiency in the areas in which they would be tutoring, viz., such subjects as Initial Teaching Alphabet (i.t.a.), traditional readings, mathematics, and physical education. This method, whatever the value for those children it spurs to special efforts in order to be selected, would likely screen out many youngsters who could benefit from being tutors.

There has not seemed to be any problem in recruiting participants. Youngsters seem to be anxious to participate, to be sure for reasons ranging from simply a desire for a change of pace—a nice way of saying "to get away from the regular teacher"—to more socially meaningful and academically acceptable reasons. Perhaps the single most important criterion for selection of the children who will be teaching is genuine interest and commitment to sustained participation.[14] These factors often may not be estimated prior to the child's beginning the program, and participation itself may be the most powerful motivator. Thus, to the maximum extent admission should be open; interest, seriousness, and desire should be the key criteria; and, perhaps, children themselves should be involved in any screening necessary.

In the Maimonides program, where sixth-grade children

12. Van Wessem, "A Tutoring Program: The Second Year," appendix 7.
13. Ibid., p. 2.
14. There are some suggestions that for an ongoing cross-age program, tutors below the fourth grade may lack the necessary maturity and willingness to make the required sustained commitment.

tutor first-graders, the tutors wrote letters to fifth-grade teachers describing the qualifications tutors should have:

> A tutor needs a lot of patience. When a child makes a mistake, the tutor cannot get excited but patiently corrects the mistake. A tutor also needs intelligence to be able to read well and make decisions. A tutor also needs the capability to teach. Last, but not least, you must be able to get along with children and have a good sense of humor but know when to be stern.[15]

Pairing

In part, the issues relating to pairing the child who is teaching and the one being taught are a function of the particular goals and strategies of the given program. For example, in Youth Tutoring Youth programs, where great emphasis is placed upon the tutor-tutee relationship, continuity of pairs is sought. On the other hand, in Woolman's program, where prime focus is upon the material to be taught, the pairs are frequently shifted. Similarly, should role modeling be seen as a key facet of the program, this should be considered when choosing pairs. For example, the Pocoima program found that while race and sex were not crucial factors for white or black children or Mexican-American girls, Mexican-American boys did not do well when the tutor was a girl. Similarly, MFY's Homework Helper program found that with children in New York City, it was better for black children if the pairs were homogeneous as to race and sex, while among Puerto Ricans and whites this did not seem to be significant.

While the desirability of seeking race and sex homogeneity is a function of program goals, in any case the pairs must provide a level of rapport sufficient that the relationship can develop. One of the factors in this rapport is the sense of confidence upon the part of the tutor that he can help the tutee.

15. Pollack, Sher, and Teitel, "Child Helps Child and Both Learn," p. 5.

It is wise *not* to match up a slow older with a very quick younger, or one too close to his own age or academic competence.[16]

It has been discovered that if the older helper is three years older (or more) than the younger he is helping, this tends to safeguard his image as older, wiser, and a resource. It also makes the younger feel it is not at all threatening for him to know less than the older who is so much older. A sixth grader, performing on a fourth grade level, can be very helpful to a second grader or even a third grader. The closer the older and younger are in age the more of an expert in the content area of help giving the older should be.[17]

The practice of operating programs has generally been to do the pairing on an informal basis—perhaps allowing for some self-selection, being attentive to problems of relationship and making shifts as necessary. While one may not want to do the weekly shifting of Woolman's program, some rotation may be useful in terms of each party learning to work with others and adjust to different styles. Another consideration is the rotation of tutor tasks. The Pocoima program found that "most tutors did not like having the same type of task for long periods; they seemed to prefer alternating between supervising groups of learners engaged in independent activities, and intensively assisting a learner on a one-to-one basis."[18]

While most tutoring has been on a one-to-one basis, there is nothing inherently limiting it to such an arrangement. A number of programs have used one to several or even one to many tutor-tutee relationships. A report on a California project notes that various ratios are possible "depending on the

16. Lippitt, Eiseman, and Lippitt, *Cross-Age Helping Program* . . . , p. 51.
17. Ibid., p. 60.
18. Newmark and Melaragno, "Tutorial Community Project: Report . . . ," p. 48.

age range difference between youngers and olders, the support and skills offered by the adults, and the intellectual and emotional levels of the children involved."[19] And not only can one tutor work with a group of tutees but occasions may arise, as in the program teaching "formula phonics" in Los Angeles, when several tutors may work with a like or larger number of tutees.[20]

Training

The extent and nature of the training is in large part a function of individual program perspective. The National Commission on Resources for Youth takes a stance of *limited pre-service training*, seeking thereby to maintain (and reinforce) the child's "naturalness" while stressing in-service training directed to the development of the tutor's inner resources. The Lippitts place great emphasis on training and have developed a design for formal pre-service and in-service training.[21] Whatever one's perspective on the amount and extent of training, and *one can do training so as to retain and strengthen "naturalness" as well as to squash it*, all programs will need to provide some pre-service orientation or training, while probably placing greater emphasis upon ongoing in-

19. Dennie L. Briggs, "Older Children Teaching Youngers," *Journal of the California Teachers Association* (January 1967), p. 76.
20. Crenshaw Community Youth Study Association, "Summer Crash Tutorial Program" (Los Angeles, California, 1968).
21. A combination of phonograph records, an accompanying training manual, a film strip, and other written material has been developed. This includes a series of ten seminars. The seminar topics suggest their content: (1) Difficulties Children Have Learning. (2) Why is School-Work Important? (3) Relationships Between Olders and Youngers. (4) Case History Analysis of a Younger Child. (5) Interview Inquiry Project with a Younger. (6) Data Analysis of Inquiry Interview. (7) Examples of Alternative Ways of Helping Youngers. (8) Ways to Help Youngers Feel Important and Successful. (9) Understanding the Teacher's Role. (10) The Seminar as a Place for Sharing Experiences and Solving Problems Related to Helping Youngers. [Lippitt, Eiseman, Lippitt, *op. cit.*, p. v]

service work with the children who are teaching. In the Lippitts' program they add, to the division of pre-service and in-service, "at-the-elbow" help, in which during the older child's first assignment an adult is present "to give encouragement or suggestions whenever there is any need for this type of support."[22]

The Maimonides Medical Center program, in which the sixth-grade tutors were trained to be "expert" in various aspects of the curriculum of their first-grade tutees, developed a two-week training program that was highly structured and programmed.[23]

YTY, which places very great emphasis upon tutor creativity and invention, begins its training cycles with various self-discovery games—making a collage of oneself, writing a paragraph about oneself, being interviewed by someone else so as to allow him to make a report about one. Crucial at this stage is to open up the children who are to teach, to encourage their inventiveness and self-reliance. As a report on the program at the Rough Rock Demonstration School (Chinle, Arizona) states:

> Tutors cannot be expected to be polished in their tutoring methods or even to have an overall grasp of what tutoring entails, before they begin tutoring. Orientation should be aimed at helping tutors to arrive at the point where they want to begin.

It is our judgment that the pre-service training of tutors be short and not overly directive. It should deal with the question of who goes where, when, and what is expected of him. For some children this is all that will be necessary for them to "give it a try," and they should be encouraged to do so. Others may want more orientation, perhaps including

22. Jeffrey Eiseman and Peggy Lippitt, "Olders-Youngers Evaluation . . . ," p. 2.
23. Pollack, Sher, and Teitel, "Child Helps Child and Both Learn."

observation of the potential tutees' classes, role plays of tutoring sessions, and planning with each other or the teacher of
initial sessions.

Given a chance to explore, to discover on their own, chil-
dren tutoring will be less likely to mimic former teachers.
The opportunities for spontaneous practices is suggested in
this report on a California program.

> I feel that the effective method that Linda [tutor] used was
> allowing Jeanne to become the teacher and she became Jeanne's
> pupil. Linda would purposefully make mistakes when Jeanne
> was using the word flash cards with her. In this way, Jeanne
> would have to correct her and tell her the right answers, prov-
> ing that Jeanne knew the correct answers as well. . . . The
> most important technique that Linda used with Jeanne was to
> present her with her own problems and let Jeanne try to cope
> with them. Again and again, I noticed Linda ask Jeanne if she
> could play with crayons or draw or go outside and play. Each
> time that Linda would do this, Jeanne would look somewhat
> annoyed but she would always think of something better and
> more constructive for Linda to do. Later I noticed that Jeanne
> was less inclined to ask Linda to let her color so much. After
> suffering the same problem herself, she finally realized Linda's
> problem and tried to help her with it.[24]

Whatever the extent of the pre-service training, it is the
responsibility of the program administration, and while that
staff may conduct a portion of it, others have contributions
to make. In the Maimonides program, the sixth-grade tutors
trained their fifth-grade successors. And in the YTY program
experienced tutors lead training groups for new tutors, as well
as for their adult supervisors.

Regardless of the length of the pre-service training, the key
training will take place once the children are engaged in

24. Briggs, "Older Children Teaching Youngers," p. 26.

teaching others. *Time*[25] *should be provided for the children who teach to meet among themselves, as well as to meet with the teachers of the children whom they tutor.*[26] Whatever the power of the helping relationship itself, it is in these sessions that the opportunity is presented to heighten the effectiveness of the program. Meeting with other children who are teaching presents opportunities to compare experiences, share techniques, and explore solutions to particular problems. YTY conducts such sessions weekly for several hours; in places where the program is an integral part of the regular school day, such sessions may be conducted by the teachers of the children who do the teaching ("sending teachers") or by the "receiving teachers." Whatever the structure, it is essential that there be opportunities for the tutors to have their suggestions and concerns heard, to be asked for their ideas, to come to feel a part of a colleagueship with the adult teachers.

At Pocoima, specific subject matter training is done by the receiving teacher. The day before the whole "sending" class is to teach, the receiving teacher may take the entire older class and tell them what she wants them to do. This may include not only specific subject matter ideas but also role playing and simulations, to improve the teaching process. Following the tutoring, there are rehash evaluation sessions usually with both sending and receiving teachers; sometimes tutees as well as tutors are included in these sessions.

One cannot assume that children "naturally" know how to teach or that they will teach well. Often, in fact, the *children mimic the worst in the teachers whom they have had*, playing out upon their pupils their own need to boss or control. The

25. Details as to scheduling will be discussed below.
26. Where the program is operated outside of the regular school day and program, as is the National Commission on Resources for Youth, the contact with the teachers may be handled by other adults, such as the paraprofessionals.

training director of a Baltimore program put it well, saying, "Think of those things that turn you off. These are the things that you don't do to your kids."[27] It is in the training and evaluation sessions, with the chance to share experience, to role-play, to simulate practice, that problems can be worked out or averted and poor practices identified and worked through.

These sessions provide an opportunity for the children to explore the processes of learning as they observe them among their pupils, to gain insight into ways in which *they may learn*, to examine the reactions of their pupils to differing inputs of their own, to develop strategies for subsequent teaching. Pocoima has tutors report their tutoring experiences to their entire class; then there is a chance for comments and suggestions from their classmates, who also tutor. In addition, the Youth Tutoring Youth program has tutors keep a daily log, which is shared at the weekly tutor training sessions. Such discussions, of course, are valuable not only in helping the tutor in his teaching role but should also have their effect upon him as a pupil; and no doubt, if the adult supervisor is sensitive, these sessions can be instructive for her, too. A concise summary of some of the purposes of the sessions for older tutors describes them as the place where

the olders learned, through discussion and role-playing episodes, how to approach youngsters constructively, and how to help youngsters to accept instruction. They learned what levels of expectation were realistic of children of a particular age, and for the individuals they were to help. They learned the techniques of correcting errors in encouraging, rather than discouraging, ways. They practiced methods for taking youngsters from the levels at which they were successful to higher levels.[28]

27. Richard H. Levine, "Reaching Out for Danny," *American Education* 6, no. 6 (July 1970), p. 23.
28. Lippitt and Lohman, "Cross-Age Relationships . . . ," p. 116.

The child who is teaching must also establish a relationship with the adult teacher of the child whom he teaches (the "receiving teacher," in the Pocoima labeling). Here the child who will teach needs to learn about the work of the class and his pupil. It is important that the receiving teacher avoid treating him as if he, too, were her pupil. In fact, very quickly, a collaborative, even peerlike relationship may grow between the teacher and the tutor, since they share a common bond, the same pupil. The likelihood of such a relationship developing, of course, depends upon the sense of security and self-confidence the adult teacher feels as a teacher, for if she feels challenged by the child who is teaching, then, instead of a sense of collaboration, it will become one of competition. And most likely the teacher will turn to treating the child who is teaching not as a collaborator but as a pupil, and thus weaken the relationship.

Issues of this sort need to be dealt with in the training of the children and of the adults.[29] Another problem that may occur also relates to the way in which the receiving teacher views the purpose of the child who comes to teach one of her pupils. If seen as an extension of the adult teacher, or as an auxiliary or nonprofessional aide, then the gains for the child who is to teach will be reduced. He will be assigned merely clerical or monitorial tasks, or if involved at all in the instructional process, restricted to rote drill and the like. Or to do just what the teacher prescribes without tapping the resources of the tutor. While there is likely to be some gain to the child who is to teach in each of these activities, the real potential of the program, especially as it relates to cognitive growth, is to be directly involved in instructional activities with another child.[30]

29. See below for training of the adults.
30. Many of the problems noted here are quite similar to those faced in introducing paraprofessionals into the classroom. There, too, the question

The children who teach need to experience and thus come to understand the process of teaching, the rewards and frustrations. At Yonkers, for example, the tutors sometimes complain that having worked hard in preparing for a lesson, it flops. Par for the course, perhaps. Older tutors complain that the younger children do not read fast enough. At Pocoima they have found that among the problems tutors had were: frequently unrealistic expectations of kindergartners' capabilities; *a tendency to do the work for the learner rather than assisting him to do it himself;* a tendency to be impatient and overly strict; difficulty in working with restless learners or with problem children.[31] And one can add to the list the danger that students will overly mimic their teachers when they teach.

Perhaps, as Alexander Mood recommends, "pedagogy, educational psychology and individual psychology would become a significant part of the elementary and secondary curriculum."[32] Or to carry Charles Silberman's recommendation at the college level to the grade school, "in addition to teaching itself [which he recommends for everyone], the study of education should be put at the heart of the liberal arts curriculum, not at its margins."[33] However one puts it, a program of this sort will succeed not merely as a result of its power as an idea but also as a consequence of the support given and training provided. The key factor in this training is for the children to have a chance to explore, to think issues

---

is whether the paraprofessional is to be a maid, an aide, or a partner. See Garda Bowman and Gordon Klopf, *Training for New Careers and Roles in the American School* (New York: Bank Street College of Education, 1969); Arthur Pearl and Frank Riessman, *New Careers for the Poor* (New York: The Free Press, 1965); Frank Riessman and Hermine Popper, *Up from Poverty* (New York: Harper & Row, 1968); Alan Gartner, *Paraprofessionals and Their Practice* (New York: Praeger, 1971).

31. Newmark and Melaragno, "Tutorial Community Project: Report . . . ," pp. 24, 26.
32. Alexander M. Mood, "Do Teachers Make a Difference?" p. 7.
33. Charles Silberman, "Murder in the Classroom, III," *Atlantic Monthly,* August 1970, p. 98.

out, to discover for themselves. For if they are overly directed, given "the answer," the potential power of the program will become atrophied. As the director of a Boston, Massachusetts, program wrote, "The role of the supervisor is to support growth rather than to control the situation."[34]

ADULT TEACHERS AND OTHER STAFF

Selection

The same division faces us here as in the case of pupils: if the program involves an entire school or district, there is no issue concerning selection of teachers; they are all in it. If, however, the program is (or begins as) one of more limited extent, selection becomes a factor. Again, as with the selection of pupils, teacher participation, where such was voluntary, has usually exceeded need. In the first year of the Pocoima program, an attempt was made to limit it to sixth-grade children tutoring kindergarten youngsters; however, pressure from other teachers led to the scrapping of the initial plan of a year-by-year, grade-by-grade expansion, so that the program was extended in the second year to all grades.

Programs such as those involving children teaching others are particularly adaptable to the utilization of paraprofessionals as key adult staff. Because it is a relatively self-contained activity, important to but not all-encompassing of the class's activities, the teacher can assign responsibility for all or part of the children-teaching-children program to a paraprofessional. The responsibility is a real one, the area is not likely to be one in which the teacher feels her expertise challenged, and the paraprofessional's special capabilities of working best

34. Sister Felicite, "Youth Tutoring Youth" (Final report submitted to The John F. Kennedy Family Service Center, Inc., Charlestown, Massachusetts, August 31, 1970), p. 31.

directly with children can be put to greatest use. Perhaps, too, where paraprofessionals are from the same community as the children, their greater "closeness" to them will have similar effects as those suggested earlier as growing out of the greater "closeness" between the tutor and tutee.

Reports from teachers who have participated in these programs indicate that they have had to change their teaching style and behavior when their students participate as either pupils or tutors. And it is one of the advantages of in-school programs that they heighten the likelihood of these changes. As a kindergarten teacher in Pocoima reports, "I feel that my role as teacher of a self-contained classroom has changed. I have learned to delegate certain responsibilities and jobs to the tutors trustingly. The change was not easy, but it has gradually improved and now I can't visualize accomplishing activities, which I feel children are 'ready for' without the additional help which the tutors provided."[35] And as a sixth-grade teacher in Pocoima said, "When your kids have been teaching other kids, it's hard, then, to get up and pontificate to them. You've got to dig deeper, challenge them more. It was tough at first but after a little while they make it a better class to teach."

Teacher Planning and Scheduling

The major operational problem of in-school programs involving children teaching other children has to do with teacher planning and scheduling. The normal elementary school with its self-contained classes provides little experience in movement of pupils from class to class. The experience in Yonkers, Pocoima, and elsewhere is that this aspect of the management threatens to overwhelm the program. Indeed, at

35. Newmark and Melaragno, "Tutorial Community Project: Report . . . ," p. 77.

Yonkers these problems have led to serious reduction in program activity, while at Pocoima they have backed off from a full-scale, school-wide "tutorial community" in favor of "sending" and "receiving" pairs. At Pocoima the "pairs" of classes have become the basic unit of the program. Once a pair of teachers has been established (the administrative staff does some "marriage-brokering"), most subsequent arrangements are made between the two teachers. Initially only a few tutors go, but as the year progresses most children in both classes participate.[36] *The key to making the system work, they feel, is time for the teachers to plan, to meet with other teachers and with pupils individually.* As one teacher at Pocoima put it in describing the problem:

Time was the detrimental factor:
a) not enough time to talk to tutors
b) not enough time to instruct tutors
c) not enough time to prepare for tutors
d) not enough time to do all that is required for the project
e) not enough time to speak with sending teachers[37]

Where the tutoring is between classes within the same school building the management problem is very much less than when it is between schools. At University City, Missouri; Cherry Creek, Colorado; Minneapolis; and San Diego, where junior high school and high school students had to go to another building to tutor elementary grade children, a combination of careful planning, heavy emphasis upon the special privilege (and inherent prestige) of being able to leave the building, and some monitoring served to assure that tutors went to their appointed sessions.[38] Perhaps the strongest factor

36. See Appendix 1 for Pocoima's "General Tutoring Plan."
37. Newmark and Melaragno, "Tutorial Community Project: Report . . . ," p. 74.
38. Indeed, the most severe discipline problem among tutors at University City occurred when one of the tutors "borrowed" a jarful of cookies from the kindergarten room for his fellow tutors!

assuring this was the realization on the part of the tutors of the sense of expectation felt by the tutees and their consequent disappointment if the tutors failed to appear. It was all summarized by an eighth-grade tutor in Lexington, Massachusetts, who went to a Cambridge elementary school to tutor.

> I liked going to teach in other schools and to have the kids learn from me and the taxi ride and listening to my radio on the way and missing classes a little bit.[39]

The tutoring, of course, means that some of the tutors may not be in their regular class for a portion of the day and may thus miss some of their "own" work. Where possible, use of time before or after the regular school day (especially possible where schools are on different time schedules), use of study or free periods, or a portion of the lunch period are ways to cut down on the incursion into "regular" school sessions. In the YTY program in San Diego, California, the junior high school students who tutor do so after the end of their school day at 1:30 P.M.; they work with groups of children in the classroom, allowing the elementary grade teachers to work individually or in small groups with the children remaining. In Athens, Georgia, where junior high school begins thirty to sixty minutes after elementary school, the tutors ride the bus with their tutees, have a hot breakfast with them at school and then tutor them. And modular scheduling, with the resultant time flexibility, enables students at Greece Arcadia High School in Rochester, New York, to tutor elementary grade pupils.

Where the tutoring is in fact part of the course work of the tutors, as in a human relations course at, for example, Cherry Creek or in the cross-age program in Detroit, then there is no loss, since the tutoring is considered field work. Where this is not the case, other arrangements can be developed.

39. LeBoeuf, "*Qui Docet Discit* . . . ," p. 56.

For example, if half the class tutors while the other is taught by their own teacher, those so taught can tutor their classmates upon their return, and the situation can be alternated. With a portion of the class away tutoring, the teacher can take advantage of the smaller number and hold individual or small group sessions with her remaining pupils. It can be a time for such activities as review, drill, special attention, individual projects, makeup, and peer tutoring. And, as a sixth-grade teacher reported, "My sixth graders come back from helping in the third and second grades so highly motivated that they learn more when they are in class than they did before. They go right to work and make up what they missed."[40] Another possibility is reported by a Washington observer: "Our 'teachers' [tutors] were so busy with tutoring they had to develop efficiency in their junior high class work."[41]

For the teacher whose students are to be taught, attention must be given to the material to be covered. The teacher becomes less the sole source of knowledge in the classroom and more of a manager of learning, an ochestrator, a resource person for both her own pupils and the children who teach. Similarly, for the sending teacher attention must be given to integrating the teaching experiences of the pupils with their ongoing work. At Pocoima, the administrators proposed a one-and-a-half-hour period twice a week for meetings between sending and receiving teachers and between each of them and their students. A mark of the program's impact is that the children's parents, when polled on releasing the children from school early in order to hold these meetings, sup-

40. Lippitt, Eiseman, and Lippitt, *Cross-Age Helping Program* . . . , p. 16.
41. Robert A. McCracken, Bernice Leaf, and Laura Johnson, "Individualizing Reading with Pupil Teachers," *Education* 86, no. 3 (November 1965): 176.

ported the idea. All schools may not find such an early release feasible; alternative ways must then be found for such planning, for without it the program tends to become too much of a hassle and is likely to dwindle.

Not only must time be available but it should be carefully chosen. In one program, the last half hour of the day was to be set aside for the entire class and the teacher to discuss the tutoring. This proved to be a bad choice, for some children were tired, others were more concerned with getting out of school, and some teachers were unwilling to have a serious work session then because they wanted the children to go home "happy"!

The question of whether a specified time should be established for the tutoring seems to be largely a function of particular local conditions. The question is somewhat skirted at Pocoima, with its pairs of teachers who have children back and forth almost throughout the entire day. In some instances individuals or groups of children go, or in other cases the entire sending class will go together. The key is the planning between the teacher pairs.

A somewhat serendipitous effect at Pocoima is that not only does the cross-age tutoring go on as part of the program, but among both sending and receiving classes children have sought and teachers have seen the value of tutoring among peers within the classes. Thus the teachers need to plan this activity, as well as the formal cross-age program. What appears to be happening at Pocoima, a program thrice favored—in its innovative co-directors, a seven-year Ford Foundation grant, and the school-wide scope—is that the basic cross-age tutoring program has opened up many other facets of the school program, viz., the teaching practices of individual teachers, the peer tutoring that has grown up within individual classes, and the beginning of a program to bring adults from the community into the school to provide specialty instruction.

Training

As with the children who are to teach, so, too, the adult teachers need training. First, of course, teachers need to be provided initial orientation in the program. While they may not have been a part of the initial decision-making process that brought the program to the school (or district), they should be brought in soon thereafter and their ideas sought out as to program details. Opportunity should be made available before the opening of the school year to provide ample time for teachers to learn about the program, to "walk through" it, to gain familiarity. If possible some phasing processes may be sought—having some teachers visit for at least a week or so an existing program or starting the program on less than a full-scale basis, either during summer school or with a few classes. That way the "bugs" can be worked out without overwhelming the system as a whole.

As with the children who teach, the training for the teachers should continue throughout the school year, providing an opportunity for teachers to meet with their peers and share and discuss problems. Such an ongoing program also offers a means for teachers who come in midyear a way to gain orientation in the program. *The heavy turnover, particularly in ghetto schools, makes this an especially important need.* Perhaps such techniques as ~ape recordings of earlier sessions, special written materials, and maybe best of all the assignment of new teachers to older ones as "buddies" could be used. Similarly, a means should be established to enable substitute teachers to carry the program ahead.

The organization of the teacher training should be informal but regular. Attention should be paid to issues perceived by the teachers, although there will presumably be some issues the program administrators will want to raise. Of course, where paraprofessionals are a part of the program they should participate fully in the training, both orientation and in-service.

Among likely teacher concerns are the feelings that by participating they will show weakness by asking for help in their job; that they will lose influence with their classes; that their colleagues will think they are trying to get out of work by passing on their teaching load to tutors; that they will "lose" their relationship to the children; that the tutors may work at cross-purposes from them. These are real concerns, the answers to which are not pat responses but require a working out over time.

The training sessions for teachers, as well as for the children, must be forums for eliminating behavior inimical to the success of the program. The central notions of a teaching role for children and the informal dimension of learning need to be conveyed. For example, at a YTY-conducted teacher training session, a "brainstorming" exercise with tutors produced fifteen suggestions when led by "rigid" teachers and over a hundred each when led by more open and flexible teachers. YTY advocates the use of teachers to train other teachers, as well as the use of successful tutors to train new teachers and administrators.

It is interesting that a study of two alternate procedures for counseling tutors by teachers—one more directive and didactic than the other—found no significant difference between the two in terms of effect upon the tutors or those whom they tutored.[42] The study, which divided the group of fifth- and sixth-grade tutors according to which of the two counseling techniques they received and then each group into high and low achievers based upon reading skills, found no

42. Stanley Frager and Carolyn Stern, "Learning by Teaching: Fifth and Sixth Graders Tutor Kindergartners in Prereading Skills" (University of California at Los Angeles, n.d.).

significant difference in effect upon tutors caused by the counseling techniques used, nor any significant difference in the effect upon the kindergarten children who were tutored in prereading skills. The significant differences that were discovered were that children tutored "were superior to the control group children who did not receive tutoring; that there was greater effect upon previously low-achieving tutors than upon high-achievers; [but] that the achievement level of the tutor seems to make little difference in the amount of learning attained by the tutee. . . ."[43]

The lesson, perhaps, of this study is that a program of youngsters tutoring others will benefit both tutor and tutee, and what the adults do (within limits) may not be decisive.

LOGISTICS

Space

Ideally, separate space should be available for the tutoring sessions. In most schools, however, this is not likely to be the case. One alternative is to build or separate off little carrels that could be used. The flexible arrangements of many early elementary school classrooms may lend themselves to this. Somewhat more elaborate are the special desks used in Woolman's program. And simpler is the arrangement worked out at the Bellevue School at Santa Rosa, California.

> I was able to group pupil desks at the front of the room, leaving five desks in areas around the back for tutoring. Large cardboard furniture boxes were cut up to form dividers between the desks. . . . Later we added paintings and pictures to the dividers and found them useful and decorative.[44]

43. Ibid., p. 5.
44. Letter, dated January 30, 1968, and Thermofaxed report, "Student-

When an entire class is being tutored at the same time, the need is for adequate space for each of the pairs, while when only a few children are involved, the problem becomes one of providing space separate from the rest of the class so as not to be disturbed by them, or vice versa. It probably is easier for the tutoring to take place in the tutee's classroom, as materials are more readily at hand.[45] However, there is surely nothing sacrosanct about the location of the tutoring, and the tutor's classroom, a lounge, a cloakroom, an empty classroom, a corner of the library, corridors, cafeteria, all could be used. What is essential is that it be a *relatively* private and quiet place, and one in which the children feel comfortable and do not see as demeaning or second class. It is probable that where the space is private, as compared to a space under the constant eye and supervision of the adult teacher, the children, or at least the tutor, will feel that a greater sense of respect and responsibility is given to him.

Tutor Program for First Graders" (n.d.), cited in Herbert Thelen, "Tutoring by Students· What Makes It So Exciting?" *The School Review* 77, no. 3 (September 1969): 229–244.

45. A study of a Michigan project including 188 sixth-grade tutors, in seeking to explain the great gains made by tutors the previous year as contrasted with lesser gains made the subsequent, cites as the key difference between the second and the first that in the second year tutoring took place in a special room rather than in the tutees' classroom, as it had the previous year. The evaluation study states: "It was concluded the key to the Cross-Aged Tutoring Program is to send the tutors to the classroom of the children they are tutoring. The enrichment of the tutor's self-concept comes from this relationship with the classroom teacher on the teacher-to-teacher basis and the audience respect and admiration of the children in the tutored child's class." [Raymond Bottom, "Report on the Cross-Age Tutoring Technique Used in a Culturally Deprived Area." (ESEA evaluation report, Waterloo and South Monroe, Michigan, Townsite Schools, April 1968), p. 4.] However interesting this conclusion, its power must be discounted by the singularity of its finding (no other program makes such a report), the smallness of the sample, and the special problems the program had in implementation ("poor coordination . . . a non-cooperative principal and less than enthusiastic teachers." [Private letter from Raymond Bottom, September 16, 1970.]).

Where a program is conducted after school, the number of places that can be used are increased considerably; not only are schoolrooms more readily available, but children can be brought to such places as community centers, libraries, and other meeting rooms. In Flat Creek, North Carolina, a very rural poverty area, tutors go to the homes of their tutees; the low attendance rate these children have means that they would not otherwise have the tutoring opportunity.

Materials

YTY *encourages the preparation of materials by the tutors.* This not only provides greater flexibility and opportunity for tutor creativity but also gives the tutors the chance to dig more deeply into the subject matter than would be the case if they were to use prepackaged material. Such work by the tutor—both in the seeking out of the material to be used and in its actual preparation—is yet another aspect of learning through teaching. If emphasis is placed upon tutor-created material, then tutors will need time, materials, and training. They will need stimulation through exposure to curriculum materials, participation in discussion groups to swap materials and ideas and in role plays to practice utilization, a place to prepare lessons where they have access to adequate materials, audio-visual materials, and resource persons to answer their questions.

Tutees' teachers will most likely want tutors to place greater emphasis upon the material actually being used in the tutees' class. For some tutees simply spending additional time on the same material may be useful. However, for others it may be that the change of pace provided by other material will be more fruitful. Perhaps what is called for is a combination of work with the regular material, use of other existing material, and material developed by the tutor or the tutor and the tutee together.

Harry Morgan has developed the notion of the "Journal of the Self," a scrapbook that each child develops about himself and uses as a device for children to teach each other both about themselves and in more substantive areas.[46] And a Washington school, short of books for its third-grade "reluctant readers," recruited seventh-graders to write original stories for their tutees.[47] In the Detroit cross-age program, one older-younger pair wrote stories about each other and the things they had done, and then they each read the other's story and commented upon it. And one older tutor and her very shy younger tutee read stories to each other over the telephone.[48] YTY recommends picture taking as a good spark to writing. Indeed, stories based upon pictures taken on a walk, stories told by tutee to tutor (and vice versa) are all means for further learning through teaching and include tutor- and tutee-developed materials. Given the spark of other creative material, the children not only use it, but more importantly, go on to create their own new material.

EVALUATION

The breadth of the goals of programs involving children teaching other children makes evaluation a complicated and complex process. Something of this range is seen in the listing of eighteen different goals for the Cherry Creek (Englewood, Colorado) project, in which high school students tutor elementary grade youngsters in science. The goals are further broken down between those for the tutors, those for the tutees, and those for the teachers.[49]

46. See the National Commission on Resources for Youth, "A Manual for Trainers" (New York: NCRY, 1970).
47. McCracken, Leaf, and Johnson, "Individualizing Reading with Pupil Teachers," p. 174.
48. Eiseman and Lippitt, "Olders-Youngers Evaluation . . . ," p. 7.
49. "The eighteen goals are as follows. (A1) High school students will

The breadth of goals involved in such programs is not the only issue; an evaluation of them must be concerned not only with long-range benefits or results but also with day-to-day operational issues, differential benefits to varying population groups (as tutors and tutees), and program variables that would affect the way in which the program is carried out on a day-to-day basis.

Evaluation designs often tend toward either of two extremes: they are highly academic, narrowly conceived schemes, often difficult to administer, or they are highly subjective, with little scientific validity. Edward Suchman has tried to strike a balance.

use inductive approaches to help children learn through the planning, preparation, presentation, and evaluation of experience-centered instructional units. (A2) High school students will respect the uniqueness of each learner, his interests, his imagination, his skills, and needs. (A3) High school students will become more sure of whether or not they desire to become teachers. (A4) High school students will exhibit an increased understanding of the structure and patterns peculiar to specific subject matter areas. (A5) High school students will be reliable in attending teaching sessions. (A6) High school students will express satisfaction with being of service to other people. (A7) High school students will accept responsibility for helping children experience success in mastering techniques and developing good craftsmanship in the use of materials.

"(B1) Each child will be directly involved in using physical materials by handling, building, observing, manipulating, experimenting, etc. (B2) Each child will improve his ability to think creatively and critically. (B3) Each child will demonstrate increased ability and freedom of self-expression. (B4) Each child will exhibit an increased willingness to help his fellow students learn. (B5) Each child will state his desire to have a high school student help him learn.

"(C1) Elementary teachers will seek the assistance of high school students to help children learn. (C2) Elementary teachers will help high school students learn how to work with elementary children. (C3) Elementary teachers will visit the senior high school on a regular basis. (C4) Project associates in cooperation with participating elementary teachers will prepare experience-centered activities for each phase of the project that are appropriate for high school students to use with elementary children. (C5) High school teachers will visit elementary schools on a regular basis. (C6) Elementary and secondary teachers will encourage other teachers and high school students at all ability and achievement levels to participate in the project." ("1970–71 Continuation Proposal for 'Mutually Aided Learning' Project, ESEA Title III" [Cherry Creek Schools, Englewood, Colorado, 1970], pp. 14–18.)

A great deal of confusion and acrimonious debate exists in the field of evaluative research today because of the failure to recognize that scientific adequacy is a matter of degree and that decisions about the rigorousness of an evaluation study must represent a compromise between scientific requirements and administrative needs and resources. . . . As one moves from the theoretical study to the evaluative study, the number of variables over which one has control decreases appreciably, while the number of contingent factors increases.[50]

Illustrative of some of the problems faced by evaluators is the experience of the Mobilization for Youth program. Cloward[51] found that while the tutors made remarkable gains in reading scores—over three years in seven months—there was no corresponding change in the children's school grades. Among the many possible explanations for this apparent inconsistency are insufficient time for the effect to show in school marks; the delayed effect of reading improvement; the limited power of reading improvement as an affecter of marks; the limited importance of reading in school; and the "Pygmalion in the classroom" expectation effect, teachers having previously identified these children as poor students and marking them as in the past, regardless of their changed performance.

Whichever of these (or other) factors are involved in this discrepancy between demonstrated reading score improvement and school marks, the phenomenon points to some of the problems involved in evaluation of these programs. As with all efforts at evaluation, those seeking to assess the effects of learning through teaching programs are well advised to establish clear and measurable objectives and institute evaluation procedures at the very beginning of the program. Be-

50. Edward Suchman, *Evaluative Research* (New York: Russell Sage Foundation, 1967), p. 76.
51. Cloward, "Studies in Tutoring," pp. 14–25.

cause of the mixed cognitive and affective goals of these efforts and the number of different participants (tutors, tutees, the adult teachers) special care should be taken to use instruments and procedures designed to tap these several levels and multiple players.

Within the cognitive area itself there are various levels of activity and consequently different measures of achievement. Achievement tests and school marks measure one set of phenomena, but we would want also to assess the degree to which the child is won to learning, is interested in learning, becomes more curious and imaginative, and learns how to learn. And if gains in these factors do not reflect in grades, one must question why not.

There are several ways in which achievement tests may be used. First, before and after tests comparing the student's previous rate of achievement with that during the time he was involved in the learning through teaching program. If the rate is markedly different during the latter period, one might feel that something had happened to his interest and skill that had not happened before. Second, one can match children by such factors as age, sex, I.Q., and peer status and then include only one member of the pair in the program. At the end one would test both members of the pair, and if there is a noticeable difference in performance and the matching is done carefully,[52] one may assume it is in part, at least, a result of the program. However, results of achievement tests might not be solely a result of increased knowledge or understanding. Rather it may "reflect a student's greater willingness to cooperate with teachers by trying to do his best on the test, where before he may not have bothered to try. A measure of

52. For example, both members of the pair should be desirous of entrance into the program to establish a control for the effect of desire on performance.

unusual growth may indicate a change of attitude rather than skill. But the program hopes to improve both, so this is still a measure of the program's effect upon the student."[53]

Various scales have been developed to measure interest in learning and sense of pleasure in school attendance.[54] Again, one can use "control" students for comparison on this subjective measure. Reports on interactions between peers and cross-age pairs, anecdotal records, interviews of participants, reports on attendance are all useful indices as well. And the cross-age project suggests a fifteen-item attitude and behavior scale that may indicate some aspects of the child's sense of self-worth.[55]

The "Cross-Age Teaching" project at the Ontario-Montclair, California, schools has sought to tap some of the many facets involved in a program of children teaching others.

Academic Learning was measured comparing experimental with control groups in achievement tests in Reading, Language, Math. for the Junior High tutors and Vocabulary, Math. and Spelling for the Elementary grade tutees. The experimental groups exceeded the control's in all areas except in mathematics.

Self-Concept was measured using the McDaniel Inferred and Self-Concept Scales. Both tutors and tutees exceeded their respective control groups.

Social Acceptability was assessed using measures of learning and leadership. Tutors' and tutees' gains exceeded that of control groups.

Discipline was measured according to teacher opinion. Both experimental groups improved more than the control groups.

53. Lippitt, Eiseman, and Lippitt, *Cross-Age Helping Program* . . . , p. 56.
54. Ibid., pp. 56 ff.
55. Ibid., Appendix A.

Attendance was increased for both tutors and tutees in comparison with the control groups.[56]

As part of its ongoing technical assistance to the Youth Tutoring Youth programs operating in more than 200 school districts, the National Commission on Resources for Youth has brought together a Research Advisory Council to develop and refine a monitoring and assessment system for YTY programs that are part of Neighborhood Youth Corps projects. While the particular location of these programs, as well as the National Commission on Resources for Youth's philosophy, gives its special angle to the program's goals, the following chart illustrates a potential model of an evaluation design developed by Fred Strodtbeck, Social Psychology Laboratory, University of Chicago, moving from hypothesis to instrument(s) to variables.[57]

TUTOR HYPOTHESIS

Hypothesis	*Instrument(s)*	*Variables*
1. Better work attitudes	New Careers Institute work ethic scale Supervisory ratings	Acceptance of work ethic Work behavior, attitude
2. Improve attitudes toward learning and school	Rotter's Internal-External Scale	Competency and environmental control vs. fatalistic subjugation to environment

56. "Cross-Age Teaching, Evaluation Summary, 1969–1970" (Ontario-Montclair, California, School District, n.d.); "Report of Evaluation of ESEA Title III Project—'Cross-Age Teaching'" (Ontario-Montclair Elementary School District, Santa Paula Elementary School District, California, July 15, 1970).

57. "Final Report on Demonstration Project Proposal to Develop a Monitoring-Assessment System for Youth Tutoring Youth E&D Model In-School NYC Program" (U.S. Department of Labor, Grant no. 42-9-12-134, June 30, 1969, to June 29, 1970), p. 26A.

	Thematic Apperception Completion	Need achievement
	Franck's Drawing Completion Test	Pragmatic self-orientation vs. idealistic other-orientation
	Boyd's Attitudes Toward School	Self-image regarding school work. Relationship to teacher. Importance of doing well
3. More positive self-image	School records	Behavior ratings
	Loevinger's Sentences	Self-concept and self-development
	Boyd's Attitudes Toward School	Confidence vs. anxiety
4. Increasing skills	School records Reading tests	Reading and achievement goals
5. Gains in vocational interests and plans	Vocational Educational planning	Vocational educational interests
	Occupational aspirations	Aspirational realities
	Postemployment evaluation questions	Employee assessment of NYC experience
6. Improved motivation	Thematic Apperception Completion	Need efficacy
	NCI Work Motivation	Motivation to work

The National Commission project has not only developed evaluative schemes, now being field-tested in several programs, but also is developing a research kit that can be administered in YTY programs.

Designs such as the above can give data for final program

evaluation. In addition, program administrators need information of a more immediate and particular nature. For
example, what is the value of tutor-prepared materials? Is it
worth the tutors' time or is it divertive from the real areas of
gain in the program and would using prepackaged materials
be just as effective?

There are questions that relate to the best staffing pattern—
should professional teachers, paraprofessionals, volunteers, or
others manage these programs? And then, who benefits most—
the underachiever, the disturbed or handicapped, boys or
girls, younger or older?

What are the best patterns of pairing tutor and tutee?
Cross-age? Cross-sex? Cross-race? Cross-background? Some
or one of these? One to one? Or one to many? Or many to
many? Are programs most effective—according to what criterion—when operated as part of the regular school day or
after school?

Obviously no single project can answer all of these questions,
or the many more that confront managers. What can be done
is to be clear about the particular goals of the specific project;
to establish some set of priorities as to those issues which are
to be evaluated; to adapt or develop evaluative instruments at
the beginning of the project; and to be aware of the research
efforts—previous and present—of similar programs.

CHAPTER VI

Conclusion:
A Strategy for Change

The evaluation of LTT from a variety of studies,[1] no one of which is conclusive by itself, indicates that it is a highly effective principle, capable of producing leaps in learning.

Learning through teaching works for a great variety of reasons, both cognitive and emotional. For the tutor, it provides feelings of competency and increased self-esteem, develops responsibility and maturity, and may even help overcome shyness. The tutor becomes an active, participating learner, filling in gaps in his previous learning, which is now reinforced by new insights. In a sense, he obtains all the benefits of overlearning.

Initially LTT may serve as contact point for the tutor, but

1. Cloward, YTY, Pocoima, Lippitts, Ontario-Montclair, etc.

as he progresses it may assist him in learning how to learn, in managing his own learning, in improving his study habits, in understanding the learning process. He may come to *expect* more of himself as a result of being placed in the teaching role. Moreover, the cooperative experience with a peer or with a younger child offers an important social experience in contrast to the competitive context in which learning generally takes place in our society. In general, teaching is brought more down to earth, is demystified, is made a regular part of a youngster's everyday experience. LTT may even assist the tutors in understanding the teacher.

For the teacher, learning through teaching provides a change of pace, is an efficient way to cover material, provides time to work with other teachers and increasingly to play the role of orchestrator or manager of learning. The teacher may come to see how she is perceived by the children from seeing them playing the teaching role. This can be very insightful and useful.

For the school, the learning atmosphere is opened up, the school program is derigidified, and more pluralistic forms of learning take place. Learning that is less formalized, sequenced, more open ended, gamelike, down to earth may result.

For the tutee, the ultimate benefit will be derived *if the tutor, as a result of his own improved learning, becomes a better tutor*. We have indicated that in most learning studies the tutee, at least on the traditional cognitive measures, improves only slightly, if at all. But if the tutor is assisted to improve his learning through LTT, and is then directed more specifically to improve his tutoring, it may be possible to produce a leap in the learning of the tutee hitherto not achieved. For this to happen, of course, the planners and managers of LTT will have to assist the tutor to utilize his new learning skills in the direction of improving his tutoring skills.

The tutee, of course, benefits from the increased individualization attendant upon learning through teaching, the closeness, the contact, the possible idiosyncratic creative adaptation of materials, the give and take, the constant immediate feedback, the attention, the chance in some cases to imitate an older peer, the increased range of learning possibilities provided by learning through teaching's potential for informal open-ended learning, and finally the opportunity to learn cooperatively, possibly in an ethnically integrated setting.

The power of learning through teaching derives from a number of different dimensions: as we have seen, it has multiple benefits—for the tutor, tutee, teacher, and school. It is relatively easy to apply at least at a minimal level, that is, within one classroom or between two teachers. It has both cognitive and emotional benefits. LTT can be applied in many different ways and settings, by people whose points of view and styles differ. It can be applied at the college level, where students teach each other, as in the McGill "learning cell." It can be applied in private industry, in the training of "hard-core" workers. It can be applied in day-care centers and prisons. It can be applied through an entire school, as at Pocoima or in Yonkers. It can be applied in after-school programs, as in Youth Tutoring Youth, or within and between schools, as in the Lippitts' cross-age learning design. The tutor can teach one child or more than one child at the same time. The tutor and tutee can reverse roles. Tutors can be poor students, average students, or good students. There can be an almost equal emphasis on the tutor's learning and tutee's learning, or the major emphasis can be on the tutor or the tutee. The tutor can receive varying degrees of training, pre-service and in-service. The learning material to be taught can be highly formalized and specific or more informal, less programmed, less sequenced, less preplanned, more gamelike. The learning sessions can take place loosely throughout the day or at designated times and places within the classroom or at some other specially designated place.

For all these reasons, learning through teaching provides the potential for a breakthrough in the learning of children. For this to happen other than on a minimal basis, however, requires careful planning, managing, leadership, and training, particularly if it is to occur on a large scale, school-wide, system-wide basis. *The LTT planners will have to utilize consciously the various mechanisms that account for the effectiveness of learning through teaching* that have been described in Chapter III. *Many of these mechanisms operate on a probability basis; that is, it is likely that they will occur, but not necessary.* Moreover, they can be blocked or derailed. For example, while it is possible that the tutor will learn how to learn, reinforce his own learning, and come to understand the teacher better, this is by no means certain. Bad preparation or inadequate training of the tutor can not only prevent these things from occurring, but can produce tutoring of a highly negative kind: the tutor may imitate some of the presumed, authoritarian characteristics of the teacher and tell a child that he had better learn or else.

The purpose then of consciousness on the part of the LTT planners is to accelerate and heighten the learning processes for both the tutor and tutee. The aim must be to both widen and deepen the learning—widen it by applying it to larger numbers of youngsters so that every youngster has the chance to play the teacher role, and deepen it by producing a higher level of learning for both the tutor and the tutee through the fullest use of the mechanisms that account for its effectiveness. This will require constant retraining of old teachers and training of new teachers, and major changes in schools of education.

BUREAUCRATIZATION VS. INSTITUTIONALIZATION

We have indicated throughout that, as learning through teaching moves from small-scale demonstration experiments to large-scale system-wide programs, there is the possibility that it will be diluted rather than accelerated. YTY has suggested a number of ways of preventing this atrophy by bureaucratization from occurring and insuring instead a positive spreading institutionalization of the program (see Chapter IV). Successful implementation depends upon five basic principles utilized by YTY: (1) a carefully developed internship program as well as a refresher course for administrators, supervisors, and other personnel; (2) the development of materials for use by the supervisors, administrators, and tutors themselves; (3) the winning of a solid commitment of the administrators to the program; (4) the careful assignment of specific people who would have as their sole responsibility the carrying out of the program at the local level; (5) the encouragement of flexible modification of the YTY design to make it applicable to specific local conditions.

The general atmosphere of accountability that today is being demanded by both the community and the experts can function as a powerful countervailing force to prevent bureaucratization. In addition, it is extremely important to develop constituencies committed to the full application of learning through teaching. These constituencies, which can be community groups, professional groups—including teachers and administrators—and, of course, the students themselves, must receive guidelines to assist them in the general monitoring of the programs. The constituencies must not only demand the fulfillment of the program but must acquire increasing knowledge regarding possible bureaucratic distortions—for example, the ways in which the climate of the school can suffocate or divert LTT.

The constituencies must be aware of the need for careful planning, training, and management on the part of the operators of the programs. They must realize that resources are required to implement the program properly, including, possibly, initial overstaffing. They must come to understand the importance of building a positive, pervasive climate for the program and the need to involve various groups, such as children, teachers, parents, and community groups, in the planning, implementation, and evaluation of the program.

The constituencies must understand the importance of phasing in the program carefully. They must see the relevance of focusing on LTT to keep it as a high priority so that other school programs are not permitted to interfere and compete. Finally, they must insist on careful follow-through, great attention to detail, and constant modification based upon flexible evaluation. In essence, some of the positive aspects of the demonstration phase must be carried over in the institutionalizing of the program.

Three Stages of Change

It may be useful to provide constituencies with a working model of the stages of change. Programs in any field go through essentially three stages:

1. The demonstration or innovation stage, which arises because of the inadequacies of the existing program functioning at the bureaucratization stage. Most LTT projects are at this innovative stage.

2. The institutionalization phase, which attempts to expand

those small-scale experimental demonstrations that have had some success. YTY is now attempting to do this in over 250 school systems.

3. The bureaucratization stage, where the institutionalized reform has now become rigidified, not attuned to changing conditions but continuing to function because of the needs of the bureaucracy rather than because of its effectiveness as a program. This in turn leads to pressure for new innovation, and the cycle may begin again.

The bureaucratic phase will resist innovation; one of the most important forms of resistance is to encapsulate or isolate the innovation as a demonstration project, thereby preventing it from becoming institutionalized. Thus the major strategic issue in changing the system is moving from the demonstration phase to the institutional phase, and this requires the overcoming of bureaucratic resistance in all its many forms.

Unless one distinguishes between the institutional and the bureaucratic phases, one is drawn inevitably to the cynical conclusion that all innovations are destroyed either by ultimately becoming bureaucratized or by being so effectively resisted by the bureaucratic culture that they never go beyond the embryonic demonstration point.

A major reason for the failure of positive institutionalization has to do with the way innovations are introduced into the educational system and *distorted by the administrative practices* of many of these systems. Failures relate to administrative lethargy, intransigence, overcontrol, poor management approaches, and lack of participatory inclusion of teachers, students, and parents.

There is typically, in addition, a lack of trained cadre to apply new innovative approaches and a lack of depth training to enable people to become cadre. The training of teachers, which has been particularly inadequate in the United States, has been badly modeled by the college training programs, which are removed from the community and the school, over-controlled by the professional associations and their dictates, to say nothing of being removed from the classroom.

A basic strategy would seem to require reducing the time spent at the bureaucratic stage, increasing the time spent at the institutional phase, and moving as rapidly as possible from innovation to institutionalization. In addition, of course, one would want the fullest development of many demonstration projects.

Successful transition, however, does not only require moving up the scale in stages. It also requires capturing and using some of the features that characterize the demonstration: *flexible* application of rules and procedures; *keying or concentrating* on the objectives of the program to the exclusion of all the various interferences or distractions that characterize school cultures (fire drills, special programs and meetings); *strong leadership* and the designation of specific personnel to take charge of the program, rather than sliding the responsibility to other people who have other responsibilities.

Related to all this is the need to develop *cadre* who understand the program, are deeply committed to it and are trained in how to implement it, and this includes administrative skills.

Thus, the job is not only to build constituencies that support LTT, but to assist these constituencies to ensure that the program is carried through to its fullest, so that there can be a real leap in the learning of children.

Appendixes

General Tutoring Plan,
Pocoima School District, Los Angeles, California

I. *Orientation Training and Supervision of Independent Activities*
  A. Fifth-Graders (First Group)
     1. Selected by own teacher—4 per class
        Criteria: Initial tutors should be leader types
     2. Receive introduction to tutoring from tutor-trainer; 3-5 days, 30 minutes per day
        a) Purposes, types of tutoring
        b) General procedures for working with a learner
        c) Role playing with tutor-trainer
        d) Role playing with each other
        e) TCP staff serves as tutor-trainer at first. School personnel takes over at later date. School person should be designated early so he can keep informed of developments
     3. Kindergarten teacher informs class of tutors—role of tutors
     4. Kindergarten teacher introduces tutors to class
     5. Tutors supervise independent activities—1-2 weeks
     6. Kindergarten teacher meets with tutors
        a) On first tutoring day, to explain supervision of independent activities
        b) Weekly, to review past week's work and to plan for the next week's work
        c) Weekly, for tutors and teachers to discuss performance and problems
        d) On-the-spot, to train tutors on specific activities and procedures
     7. Additional training by tutor-trainer, when necessary
  B. Fifth-Graders (Second Group)
     1. Follow similar steps as fifth-graders (first group)
        a) Selected by own teacher—4 per class
        b) Receive introduction to tutoring

    c) Kindergarten teacher introduces tutors to class, after first group is functioning smoothly

    d) Kindergarten teacher meets with tutors—first day, weekly, on-the-spot

  2. Supervise independent activities—2 weeks

C. Evaluation of Tutors

  1. By tutor-trainer at end of training

  2. By teacher, during supervision of independent activities. Use a standard rating form

II. *Tutoring for Specific Instructional Objectives.* Kindergarten teachers see and react to materials and procedures prior to implementation

A. Fifth-Graders (First Group)

Inexperienced tutors on initial objectives

  1. Receive training on specific objectives from tutor-trainer—1 week

    a) Purpose, materials, procedures

    b) Demonstration by tutor-trainer

    c) Role playing with trainer

    d) Role playing with each other

  2. Tutors observe demonstration by kindergarten teacher in front of whole class, or part of class, as appropriate

  3. Practice tutoring with kindergarten learners—1 week

    a) 1 tutor, 1–2 learners

    b) Kindergarten teacher observes practice tutoring

  4. Kindergarten teacher meets with tutors

    a) At end of practice tutoring, to make recommendations

    b) On-the-spot, to deal with specific problems

    c) Weekly conferences

Experienced tutors with new objectives and materials

  1. Similar to prior objectives

    a) Demonstration by kindergarten teacher in front of whole class

    b) Tutors receive materials for review on own

  2. Different from prior objectives

    a) Tutor receives training from tutor-trainer as necessary

B. Fifth-Graders (Second Group)

  1. Receive training on specific objectives—1 week

    a) One at a time. Released from supervision of independent activities

b) Trained by tutor-trainer

c) Later, fifth-graders trained by experienced tutors

2. Practice tutoring, under observation of experienced tutor and kindergarten teacher—1 week

C. Evaluation of Tutors

III. *Ongoing Tutoring*

A. Types of Tutoring

1. Supervision of independent activities

2. Tutoring for specific objectives

3. Tutors alternate between the two types

B. Assignment of Individual Learners to Tutors*

1. Each tutor is assigned 3-4 learners in one class

2. Kindergarten teacher and tutor-trainer make assignments, based on strengths and weaknesses of tutors that were observed during training, and based on kindergarten teacher's knowledge of kindergarten learners

C. Testing of Learners

1. Tutor pre-tests his own learners for each specific objective, before beginning tutoring for that objective

2. Tutor tests his own learners for mastery of an objective, whenever the tutor feels the learner is ready

3. When necessary, an especially designated tutor will administer mastery tests, to take load off a tutor

D. Record Keeping

1. At first, records kept by kindergarten teacher, so that tutors do not become overloaded

2. When tutors have had experience and are comfortable with tutoring, the tutors and learners will keep own record of progress on prepared forms

IV. *Suggested Activities in Sending Class*

A. Teacher-tutors weekly conference

B. Tutors share experience with class. Teacher and tutors discuss problems with class, and solicit class suggestions

C. Tutors bring kindergarten children to fifth-grade class to meet older students and tell what they do together

---

* Assignment of a tutor to work individually with one or two learners over an extended period of time is expected to facilitate (1) establishment of personal relationship between tutor and learner; (2) tutor-kindergarten teacher communication concerning specific learners; (3) record keeping by learner and tutor and training and supervision of same by teacher; (4) compatible matching of tutors and learners.

D. Tutors post pictures of kindergarten students in class
E. Sending teacher integrates with English by relating writing assignments to tutoring (e.g., tutors may keep daily log—highlights, not detailed)
F. Sending teacher exchanges class for an hour with kindergarten teacher. Kindergarten teacher explains kindergarten program, schedule, materials; tells what kindergarten children are like and what goals of kindergarten year are; solicits and answers questions
G. Half of fifth and one-half of kindergarten class exchange students for one-one tutoring involving all fifth-graders
H. Sending teacher may supervise training of tutor by other tutor on specific objectives and materials
V. *Schedule (All Tutors Are Fifth-Graders)*

Week 1   a) Group 1 tutors selected
           b) Group 1 tutors receive orientation training
Week 2   a) Group 1 tutors supervise independent activities
           b) Group 2 tutors selected
           c) Group 2 tutors receive orientation training
Week 3   a) Group 1 tutors receive training on specific objectives
           b) Group 2 tutors supervise independent activities
Week 4   a) Group 1 tutors tutor for specific objectives
           b) Group 2 tutors supervise independent activities
Week 5   a) Group 1 tutors supervise independent activities
           b) Group 2 tutors receive training on specific objectives
Week 6   a) Group 1 tutors supervise independent activities
           b) Group 2 tutors tutor for specific objectives
Week 7   a) Tutoring and supervision ongoing with eight tutors for each kindergarten class. Each tutor assigned to 3–4 kindergarten learners.

Information on Staff and Youth Positions, National Commission on Resources for Youth, New York City, New York

Title	Background/Experience	Duties	Training
Administrator	Teacher, or educational administrator	Establish program in city or region; Obtain funds; Contact NYC for job stations; Train supervisors to lead centers	By NCRY at Internship Workshop, or by someone else familiar with Youth Tutoring Youth
Supervisors	Teachers, community leaders, or older NYC enrollees (all three kinds of supervisors have proved effective)	Run a tutorial center—daily basis; Train tutors: pre-service and in-service; Arrange for personal remediation for tutors	By administrator, or by special trainer(s) chosen by the administrator
Aide	Older NYC member, or community member	Share duties with supervisor	By administrator (usually trained along with supervisor)

(cont'd)

Tutors	In-School NYC enrollees underachieving in school	Tutor younger child(ren)	By supervisor
Tutees	Elementary age children who need tutoring	Come to tutoring sessions	By tutors (training-tutoring)

Ontario-Montclair (California) School District Cross-Age Teaching, Evaluation Summary, 1969/70

Academic Learning

A positive improvement for the experimental students over the control students was made in five of the six areas measured. (Reading, Language, and Math for the Jr. High Students and Vocabulary, Math, and Spelling for the Elementary Students.) Specifically, results were as follows:

Jr. High—Olders

The Cross-Age Teaching students exceeded the mean growth of the older control groups by 2 months or more in reading, math, and language during the seven-month period.
- Reading scores exceeded controls by 3 months;
- Math scores exceeded controls by 3 months;
- Language scores exceeded controls by 2 months.

Elementary—Youngers

The Cross-Age students receiving help exceeded the mean growth of the control groups in Language and Reading. In mathematics each group gained 8 months during the 7-month test period.
- Reading scores exceeded controls by 2 months;
- Language scores exceeded controls by 1 month.

Statistical significance was reached at the 1% level in Reading at both levels and the 5% level was reached in Language for the older students. About 75% of the students tutored received the majority of their tutoring in Reading as requested by the receiving teachers.

It should be noted that both the younger and older students in the program had a lower mean I.Q. and Grade placement scores when entering the program than did the control group of students selected.

Self Concept

It was the objective of project planners that the mean improvement in the self concept of the youngers and olders would exceed that of the control groups by at least .50 pt. on the McDaniel Inferred and Self Concept Scales. This objective was met by all groups. The younger tutored children exceeded their controls by 1.4, the Olders by 5.69, according to teacher ratings on the Inferred Scale. The Youngers exceeded their comparison groups by 5.22 and the Olders exceeded by 5.39 on the pupil-rated Reported Self Concept Scale.

These data reflect a strong change in self concept on the part of participating students, and the teachers of these pupils identified the same strong change.

Social Acceptability

On Sociometric ratings for learning and leadership, both older and younger experimental groups increased in acceptability by their peers while all comparison groups declined. The growth gained by each group is as follows:

Younger Leadership	+2.90
Learning	+3.99
Older Leadership	+5.0
Learning	+3.55

+3.0 was the desired growth set forth by project staff.

Discipline

It was the goal of project staff that 25% of the experimental older and younger children will have improved more in discipline, according to teacher opinion, than the children in the control group during the cross-age teaching period.

- The olders exceeded the control group by 6% positive gains.
- The youngers exceeded the control group by 23% positive gains.

Both of these gains are considered statistically significant at the 1% level of confidence, but did not reach the staff goal. It is believed that the 25% goal is extremely high.

Attendance

The youngers in the project significantly reduced their absences as compared with the control groups. The percentage nonattendance was 5.71% for project students and 6.44% for the comparison group. This is significant at the 1% level of confidence.

The older students had an 8.33% of nonattendance as compared to 6.58% for the control students.

The Cross-Age Teaching program has shown many positive actions: Underachievers have been motivated to learn and have met success; olders have reinforced and improved their academic learning by teaching others; students have become intimately involved in the learning process, improving both their own self-concept and their image with their peers; students have had the opportunity to experience a positive relationship with school, and have participated in learning through cooperation.

Cherry Creek (Colorado) Schools Evaluation Design

A1. *High school students will use inductive approaches to help children learn through the planning, preparation, presentation, and evaluation of experience-centered instructional units.*

Assessment of the degree of attainment of this objective will be through the systematic collection of information by the elementary teacher in charge of the children with whom the learning assistant is working and by the project associate in charge of that particular subject area. An elementary teacher checklist and a project associate checklist containing specific items designed for this purpose, along with other items designed for the assessment of objectives described below, will be completed for each learning assistant at the end of each unit.

2. *High school students will respect the uniqueness of each learner, his interests, his imagination, his skills, and his needs.*

The elementary teacher checklist and the project associate checklist will contain items calling for the elementary teacher and project associate to evaluate the degree to which the learning assistants have reached this goal.

3. *High school students will become more sure of whether or not they desire to become teachers.*

Assessment of this objective, as well as several other objectives, will be conducted by means of a learning assistant's opinionnaire, which will be administered as both a pre- and post-measure. The items will require not only an indication of their views of teaching as a career but the degree to which they believe they are able to more fully evaluate their interest in and aptitude for teaching.

4. *High school students will exhibit an increased understanding of the structure and patterns peculiar to specific subject matter areas.*

A measure of the change in understanding of the structure and patterns of the various subject matter areas will be acquired by a pre- and post-administration of an achievement test specifically constructed for this purpose. The instrument will be constructed by the project associates and administered during the first two weeks and the last two weeks of each semester.

5. *High school students will be reliable in attending teaching sessions.* Complete records of the learning assistants' attendance will be maintained by the elementary teachers using a form provided by the project director for this purpose.

6. *High school students will express satisfaction with being of service to other people.*
The learning assistant opinionnaire will include items of a Likert type composing a scale designed to measure the degree of this satisfaction.

7. *High school students will accept responsibility for helping children experience success in mastering techniques and developing good craftsmanship in the use of materials.*
The elementary teacher checklist and project associate checklist will contain items designed to measure attainment of this objective.

B1. *Each child will be directly involved in using physical materials by handling, building, observing, manipulating, experimenting, etc.*
Information pertaining to the assessment of this objective will be obtained from three sources: the elementary teacher and project associate checklists as well as a checklist which will be maintained by the learning assistants. At the conclusion of each unit, the learning assistant will complete a checklist which provides information about the degree to which each child was directly involved with the physical materials. This checklist will also contain items pertaining to objectives given below.

2. *Each child will improve his ability to think creatively and critically.*
The learning assistant checklist will contain items in which the learning assistant will be expected to indicate the degree to which improvement has taken place for each child.

3. *Each child will demonstrate increased ability and freedom of self-expression.*
The learning assistant checklist will contain items in which such increases can be noted. Provision will be made for the learning assistant to indicate specific examples of student behavior which would indicate the presence or absence of such change.

4. *Each child will exhibit an increased willingness to help his fellow students learn.*

The learning assistant checklist will contain items pertaining to such changes.

5. *Each child will state his desire to have a high school student help him learn.*

The degree to which the children desire to have the assistance of high school students will be ascertained by the elementary teacher in each classroom. Following each unit in which the learning assistant worked with the children, the teacher will poll the students by means appropriate to the particular grade level to determine the number of children out of the total in the classroom who desire to have this assistance.

C1. *Elementary teachers will seek the assistance of high school students to help children learn.*

The learning assistant opinionnaire will contain items of the Likert type designed to obtain the learning assistants' judgment of the degree to which the elementary teacher with whom they were working sought their assistance in helping children learn.

2. *Elementary teachers will help high school students learn how to work with elementary children.*

The learning assistant opinionnaire will contain items designed to determine the degree to which elementary teachers provided this assistance as perceived by the learning assistants.

3. *Elementary teachers will visit the senior high school on a regular basis.*

The project director will maintain a record of every visit of the elementary teachers to the secondary schools.

4. *Project associates in cooperation with the participating elementary teachers will prepare experience-centered activities for each phase of the project that are appropriate for high school students to use with elementary children.*

Assessment of this objective will be obtained by observation of the extent to which the desired products are produced. By September 1 the following materials should be available: training materials for the learning assistants, instructional objectives and corresponding units for the elementary children, and a schedule of activities for the school year.

5. *High school teachers will visit elementary schools on a regular basis.*

A record of the number of visits made will be maintained by the project director.

6. *Elementary and secondary teachers will encourage other teachers and high school students at all ability and achievement levels to participate in the project.*

The degree to which the elementary and secondary teachers will provide this assistance is largely determined by their satisfaction with and belief in the merits of the MAL project. Assessment of this objective, i.e., determination of the degree to which elementary and secondary teachers are in favor of and are convinced of the merits of the MAL program, will be accomplished through an anonymous questionnaire which will be administered to all teachers in the school district at the end of the school year. This questionnaire will thus provide a measure of the overall opinion of the MAL project on the part of the teachers in the school district at the end of the three-year program. It will be sent by mail to all teachers in the district with a follow-up system that will preserve the anonymity of responses as well.

Mary, a Tutor*

(Following is an ex-post-facto survey of a typical Youth Tutoring Youth tutor. Mary, age 15, was chosen for a number of reasons: [1] since she had been in the program for nearly a year [February–June 1968; July–August 1968; September 1968–February 1969], it was assumed that she has been more deeply affected than a tutor who was in the program for only a few months; [2] she had worked in the same center for the entire time [some tutors were shifted from one center to another because several centers discontinued operation at the end of the summer]; [3] since she had attended the same school that her center was located in for part of the time [February 1968–May 1968] and had attended this school since kindergarten, her teachers knew her well and could give in-depth information and comparisons of development. [Most tutors do not tutor in their own school because elementary schools do not usually extend through the eighth or ninth grade]; [4] her elementary school guidance counselor recommended her as a tutor who had needed the program most in the beginning and had been noticeably affected by participation.)

1. Interview with Mary's guidance counselor

(The following is an interview with the counselor who had originally directed the screening and selection of the tutors for the center in which Mary tutored. Because the program was held in the school that Mary attended for part of the time, an elementary school for K–8, this counselor had a chance to observe Mary within the regular school setting as well as during the after-school tutoring program. He knew Mary quite well from her previous years at the school, and was equipped to observe and perceptively analyze any changes in Mary's behavior and academic performance.)

* From NCRY, "Youth Tutoring Youth—It Worked," p. 8.

Interviewer: Could you tell me something about the home and family of Mary?

Counselor: Mary comes from a very loquacious, outgoing family. Her mother is a large woman who assumes the leadership or chairmanship of the block. She's a very domineering person, and I think Mary gets all of her moves from her mother. I can remember many instances in which things have happened here in school such as gang warfare and things of this nature and the mother has actually led the battlers; this is what I mean when I say she's an outspoken person. There is no father in the home. The family is on DPA and no one else is supposed to be in the home other than the mother. There are no boys in the family. Mary has five sisters.

I: Can you give me some background on Mary before she entered the program?

C: Mary was not doing well in school at all. I don't know whether or not you have seen her . . . she's quite a large girl. She has had a great deal of difficulty with the teachers because of her dress. She keeps up with the mod styles and with her size, she looks ridiculous. Her attitude prior to her involvement in the program was nasty. She was very difficult to reach. She was sent to the office numerous times for her behavior because of insulting remarks to other children and to her teachers. Her mother was called in and we discussed her behavior. We discussed what we expected from her, what we expected from the home and this did not bother the mother one iota. Mary had a record of truancy which started in the latter part of 1966. She began to go around with some girls who were truanting and, being a very large girl, I suppose any man would take her for being much older than she is. I talked to Mary on several instances about her attendance. She told me that she had been ill but she would never tell me that she was skipping school. The mother was called in, and, apprised of what was going on, she would give no reason of why her daughter was out of school. However the mother felt that even though Mary was not in school she must have been out for some good reason. The mother would not punish her. The mother was behind the child even though the child was clearly wrong. This is the kind of camaraderie they have in the family.

I: What was Mary's response to being chosen as a tutor for the YTY program?

C: When her name was placed on the list, Mary's homeroom teacher felt that Mary, being a very large girl, would have some impression on the children and we decided to try her in the program. We talked with Mary prior to her being placed with the children and asked her how she felt. She was overjoyed.

I: Did you notice any changes in Mary's outward behavior during the course of the program?

C: After a month or so of working with the tutees, there was somewhat of a change. It was slow but I think she put on an air of dignity. Her appearance changed for the better . . . the program gave her an older outlook. Before this period, she was always fighting or squawking or talking. After her involvement with the program, this changed. I could see her coming into the building and her entire outward appearance appeared to be that of a much older person. Now I attribute some of this to a change of schools (Mary entered the ninth grade in the fall of 1968 and therefore moved into a junior high school) and some of her involvement in the program. She has the ability. Working as a tutor in this program has done something for her—it raised her sights. Now she was saying, "I have someone depending on me," and this has helped her because she needs recognition and responsibility.

2. *Interview with Mary's homeroom teacher*

(The following is an interview with Mary's homeroom teacher in the elementary school. The teacher's classroom was located across from the rooms in which the after-school tutoring took place. Hence, he had the opportunity of observing Mary while she tutored as well as in his own class.)

Teacher: I had Mary in my homeroom all last year, 1967–1968. Mary was a pleasant child in my class simply because she liked me as a teacher. However, she had a trait which was quite obvious to other teachers. If she disliked a certain teacher or a certain subject, she would balk. At these times, she would become quite unbearable in the classroom. A lot of teachers had problems with her. As for her family life, I believe her Dad died in the military service. Mary was quite dependent on her mother and I think the lack of a father at home also added to the problems she had in school.

Mary is a big girl. A lot of the younger and smaller girls look up to her and she likes this, but if a situation arises in which she is overlooked, such as a class nomination of officers or a committee picked to supervise a party, she feels slighted. She wants to be recognized by her peers and by her elders. She seems to enjoy working with the program and she seems to like the idea that these youngsters look up to her. Mary needed recognition from the outside.

Speaking with Mary a few weeks ago, I noticed a change in her attitude that I thought was for the better. She seemed to feel that she was accomplishing quite a bit in working with the youngsters. I've noticed a motherly instinct in her and this makes tutoring an ideal job.

3. *Interview with Mary's team leader (supervisor)*

(The team leader was a 17-year-old Neighborhood Youth Corps girl who lived in the same neighborhood with Mary and knew her before the center opened.)

Team Leader: Mary, she gets along with children very well. Her main problem is that she wants attention. That's her main problem right there, attention. But she gets along with children. She's very nice. She'll do anything for you but . . . I remember this summer for instance, usually I let the tutors take the children to the play-ground and teach the tutees how to use cameras. Mary didn't want to have her picture taken with the children but she wanted to have it taken alone. We put our pictures in a book and she wanted to be in the book by herself.

I think her main problem is that she looks older. She tells everybody she's about seventeen.

I met Mary before I ever started this program. She's the only person I ever really knew in here. I knew Mary . . . like me and her were going to be buddy, buddy. She's friends with one of my best girl friends, and all of us worked here so that was another problem. I couldn't let her get away with a lot of things even though she was my friend.

Mary likes responsibility as long as she's going to get something out of it . . . like everybody does. She came to work regularly. She wants everybody to praise her but what tutor is going to praise another tutor? She would cry sometimes. I don't know why. I know she has family problems, but I don't know too much about them. Sometimes she feels everybody doesn't love her and things like that.

I think the program helped Mary. She needs somebody to have authority over and she needs somebody she can talk to. She has come and talked to me about things that she doesn't talk to anybody else about. She has a lot of problems that girls her own age don't have. She was depressed a lot and I'm the kind of person if you tell me something and you don't want anybody to know, I won't tell them. But she had a hard time adjusting with the other tutors. She wants everyone to look up to her. She wants to be like a big shot. She wants her and me to be so close that she can come in ten or fifteen minutes late or leave early and I won't say anything. I let her get away with a lot at first and then I started cracking down on her and telling her she couldn't do this and she couldn't do that.

Last year, everyone hounded me to get rid of her but I was determined. Well, I mean, that closeness was there with all of them, but there's some you can get closer to than others and Mary was one of these, I guess.

4. *Interview with Mary*

Mary: Tutoring was always easy for me. I knew all the kids. I've lived in the neighborhood and know them all well. Lots of the kids would want to be with me rather than with the other tutors. I'd come even if there wasn't pay because I like children.

Now I hate school. I used to like it, but I don't like it any more. In my new school the kids fight 24 hours a day. In each class you go to they're fighting. The boys in the lunchroom threw chocolate milk all over my gym teacher and spaghetti too. They're always arguing. I really don't think that I'm going to make it through high school. I enjoyed being in the elementary school because I was there since kindergarten and I really liked it. I hated to leave. This new school is like a house on a haunted hill.

Last spring I liked school but I seemed to have more fun after I started tutoring. I liked being around the tutors more. In the beginning I started off with two tutees and by the end I could work with six or nine; if a tutor wouldn't come, I'd take the extra tutees.

I let the kids read because I thought they should do what they liked. I think it helped me in my school work, because at night when I would go home and do *my* homework, I'd find the same things that I was teaching them.

I've always wanted to be a kindergarten teacher. Before I even started, on Saturdays I used to go into the neighborhood and get children to come and sit in my living room . . . we'd read and things.

I'd even like to start a tutoring program of my own. I can sit and talk to the kids and they listen. Just like the little girl down the hall. She didn't like her tutor so I would take her into my room and we'd sit and talk. The other kids that I had were making Christmas things, and I told her to bring a bleach bottle so she could help. Ever since that she would come where I was.

I think this is the kind of program people should know about. It is something new in this neighborhood and there's a lot of things that girls need to know about. People need to talk to somebody. . . .

Conclusions

The question that naturally follows is did the program succeed for Mary? Did it, for this particular tutor, achieve what it set out to do? How or how not? Here we must keep in mind Dr. Suchman's statement:

> Just as "complete" explanation is never possible in nonevaluative research because of the multiplicity of intervening variables with relationships being given in terms of probabilities, so absolute program effectiveness is also impossible and success becomes a matter of degree.*

At most, we can pick out of the interviews some statements and observations that relate to the stated goals. A more rigorous content analysis is more scientific but impractical for our purposes.

Did the program "promote better work habits and ways to handle responsibility?" All three of the interviewees described Mary as someone who needed responsibility, recognition, and attention. Because she was a physically mature girl and also a motherly girl who liked to give advice to younger people, the program seemed to offer Mary a natural role. In short, tutoring gave her a chance to reinforce her strong points. The job experience increased her inclinations toward teaching and perhaps made such a career more feasible. The fact that she always attended the program, whereas she had not attended school regularly, indicates that she was learning how to assume responsibility, especially when the responsibility was personally meaningful.

Were Mary's attitudes toward learning and school improved? This is more difficult to discern from the interviews. By Mary's own admission, "Last spring I liked school anyway but I seemed to have more fun after I started tutoring. I liked being around the tutors

* Suchman, *Evaluative Research,* p. 175.

more. . . . I think it helped me in my school work, because at night when I would go home and do *my* homework, I'd find the same things that I was teaching them." On the other hand, Mary stated that she hated her new junior high school. "I really don't think that I'm going to make it through high school. I enjoyed being in elementary school because I was there since kindergarten and I really liked it. I hated to leave. This new school is like a house on a haunted hill."

It is conceivable that, for Mary, the program had what Suchman calls "boomerang" (or unintended) side-effects. We know that schools are not utopias, particularly in the ghetto. The interviewer visited Mary's new school to look up her academic record. The junior high school was quite different from the elementary school which Mary had attended and which housed the YTY program. The new school was larger and older with the halls reverberating to the sound of renovations and traffic. The guidance counselor, who had a case-load of 400 and saw only extreme problems, hardly knew Mary.

Furthermore, the school was not in Mary's neighborhood. She, along with 150 other ninth-graders from West Philadelphia, were bussed to North Philadelphia schools for the ninth grade only because schools in their own neighborhood were overcrowded. Moving required quite an adjustment for Mary. It is possible that returning daily to tutor at her elementary school made Mary more intolerant and hostile towards her new school. At any rate, Mary stated that she did enjoy eighth grade more while she was tutoring and did seem to feel that her homework was more meaningful when she had to keep up with her tutees.

Did the program foster a more positive self-image for Mary? Self-image is a vague phrase, hard to define, harder to determine. According to descriptions of Mary's outward behavior, she felt better about herself. As her counselor remarked, "It was slow but I think she put on an air of dignity. . . . I could see her coming into the building and her entire outward appearance appeared to be that of a much older person. . . . Now she was saying, 'I have someone depending on me,' and it raised her sights." Mary's expressions of pride in her work, her confidence in herself as a tutor, her pride that the children liked her can be conceived as evidence that the program gave her a better sense of herself.

Finally, did the program increase Mary's skills in reading and writing? The interviews gave no evidence so information was sought elsewhere. Mary was given the Metropolitan Achievement Test in

February 1968 before she entered the program. According to norms set by the publishers of the test, Mary was then reading at a 3.6 level. In May, Mary was given the same test and by the same standards, the test showed her reading at a 4.7 grade level. If the test scores are valid, Mary gained 1.1 years in 4 months but still was not reading at her own grade level. In August 1968 she was given the IOWA silent reading test and showed no improvement. This could be due to the fact that a different test was administered and that the two tests do not exactly correlate on the norm-scale used. Viewing test scores alone, Mary did show some improvement in reading. We have no samples to determine equivalent progress in her writing skills.

In summary, the interviews indicate that YTY was a meaningful experience for Mary. It gave her a chance to achieve the recognition and responsibility that she needed. It made a possible career in teaching seem more feasible. It gave her a chance to function in a role for which she was particularly suited. In addition, the program seemed to satisfy a need in Mary for "someone to talk to." Mary seemed to find in her center leader the responsive ear of someone older yet not too old. She also saw herself in the role of providing that "someone" to younger girls. "I think this is the kind of program people should know about. It is something new in this neighborhood and there's a lot of things that girls need to know about." It is clear that the program met a need in Mary for intimacy and interpersonal contact.

Teacher's Evaluation of Tutor*

Mechanics
1. Is the tutor always punctual to class?
2. Does the tutor attend class regularly?

Attitude
1. Does your tutor ever show impatience toward students?
2. How does the tutor work with you in planning and teaching?
3. Does the tutor take sides during a disagreement between the teacher and students?
4. Does he tend to give you the idea that he enjoys his work or does he give you the idea that he has to do it?
5. What is the tutor's reaction to outbreaks of violence in the class?

Teaching Ability
6. How does the tutor handle the class when the teacher is absent or while momentarily taking over?
7. What kinds of methods does your tutor employ in teaching students?
8. How much success does the tutor have in motivating a student?
9. Does the tutor make it easier for the students to understand the work when they are in doubt? If so, how?
10. Is the tutor too forceful or not forceful enough toward the students?
11. What was the main job of your tutor? Did he fulfill this job as best he could?
12. Can your tutor work with any kind of student? (slow, fast, black, white, etc.)
13. Do you think that your tutor should be one of the fall tutors?

* From M. McCloskey, ed., *Teaching Strategies and Classroom Realities* (Englewood Cliffs, N.J.: Prentice-Hall, 1971). This questionnaire was constructed for the teachers by a committee of tutors.

Miscellaneous
14. Would you have any objection to having this paper read by your tutor?

Thank you.

Teacher's name ....

Tutor's name ....

Subject ....

Comments

Bibliography

Abt, Clark. *Serious Games*. New York: Viking Press, 1970.

Anderson, Hugh. "The Southall Project." Youth Tutors Youth, A C/S/V Report, Community Service Volunteers, London, England, n.d.

Bartholomew, Lucy, and Gurley, Heather. " 'Youth Tutoring Youth' in South Phoenix: Results and Accomplishments," August 20, 1970.

Bell, Andrew. *Bell's Mutual Tuition and Moral Discipline*. London: C. J. G. and F. Livingston, 1832.

Bell, S. E., Garlock, Norene L., and Colella, Sam L. "Students as Tutors: High Schoolers Aid Elementary Pupils." *The Clearing House* 44, no. 4 (December 1969): 242–244.

"Benefits Reported by Users of Cross-Age Helping Programs." Center for Research on Utilization of Scientific Knowledge, University of Michigan, n.d.

Bledsoe, Joseph, and Garrison, Karl G. "The Self-Concept of Elementary School Children in Relation to Their Academic Achievement, Intelligence, Interests, and Manifest Anxiety." U.S. Office of Education Cooperative Research Project no. 1008.

Bottom, Raymond. "The Effect of Tutorial Experiences on Pupil Tutor and Tutored Pupil in Intelligence, Achievement, and Social-Psychological Adjustment in Twenty Culturally Deprived Children." Monroe, Michigan, Public Schools, n.d.

———. "Report on the Cross-Aged Tutoring Technique Used in a Culturally Deprived Area." ESEA Evaluation Report, Waterloo and South Monroe, Michigan, Townsite Schools, April 1968.

Briggs, Dennie L. "Older Children Teaching Youngers." *Journal of the California Teachers Association* (January 1967): 24–26.

Bronfenbrenner, Urie. *The Two Worlds of Childhood: U.S. and U.S.S.R.* New York: Russell Sage Foundation, 1970.

Brookover, William, Shailes, Thomas, and Peterson, Ann. "Self-Concept of Ability and School Achievement." *Sociology of Education* 37, no. 3 (Spring 1964): 271–278.

Bruner, Jerome S. *The Process of Education.* New York: Vintage Books, 1963.

Caditz, R. "Using Student Tutors in High School Mathematics: Weak Students Profit From Volunteer Assistance." *Chicago School Journal* 44, no. 7 (April 1963): 323–325.

Cloward, Robert. "Studies in Tutoring." *The Journal of Experimental Education* 36, no. 1 (Fall 1967): 14–25.

Coleman, James. *Equality of Educational Opportunity.* Washington, D.C.: U.S. Office of Education, 1966.

Comenius, John Amos. *The Great Didactic.* Translated by M. W. Keatinge. London: A. and C. Black, Ltd, 1921.

Crenshaw Community Youth Study Association. "Summer Crash Tutorial Program." Los Angeles, California, 1968.

"Cross-Age Teaching, Evaluation Summary, 1969–1970." Ontario-Montclair, California, School District, n.d.

Delaney, A. A. "Good Students Help Deficient Pupils." *School Activities* 35, no. 2 (October 1963): 36.

"District Experience Learning Through Tutorial and Aide Programs." Norwalk-La Mirada, California, Public Schools, n.d.

Do Teachers Make a Difference?: A Report on Recent Research in Pupil Achievement. Washington, D.C.: U.S. Office of Education, 1970.

Eiseman, Jeffrey, and Lippitt, Peggy. "Olders-Youngers Evaluation: Covering the First Semester." Report to the Stern Family Fund and the Detroit Public School, Center for Research on Utilization of Scientific Knowledge, University of Michigan, February 1966.

Felicite, Sister. "Youth Tutoring Youth." Final report submitted to The John F. Kennedy Service Center, Inc., Charlestown, Massachusetts, August 31, 1970.

"Final Evaluation of ESEA Title III Project #6138, Cross-Age Teaching, 1969–1970," Ontario-Montclair, California, School District, July 15, 1970.

Fisher, Renee B. "Each One-Teach One Approach to Music Notation." *Grade Teacher* 86, no. 6 (February 1969): 120.

Fleming, J. Carl. "Pupil Tutors and Tutees Learn Together." *Today's Education* 58, no. 7 (October 1969): 22–24.

Fowle, William Bentley. *The Teachers' Institute*. New York: A. S. Barnes, 1866.

Fox, R. S., Lippitt, R., and Lohman, J. E. "Teaching of Social Science Material in the Elementary School." Final report, Cooperative Research Project, E–011, U.S. Office of Education, n.d., Chapter 5.

Frager, Stanley, and Stern, Carolyn. "Learning by Teaching: Fifth and Sixth Graders Tutor Kindergartners in Prereading Skills." University of California at Los Angeles, n.d.

Galvin, John, and Shoup, Mary Lynn. "The Use of Peers in Teaching Reading to Withdrawn Children." U.S. Office of Education Grant G3-06-062063-1559, n.d.

Glasser, William. *Schools Without Failure*. New York: Harper & Row, 1969.

Goldschmid, Marcel L. "Instructional Options: Adopting the Large University Course to Individual Differences." *Learning and Development* 1, no. 5 (February 1970). Center for Learning and Development, McGill University.

Gordon, Patricia. "Olders Tutor Youngers Evaluation." Flat Creek, North Carolina, August 10, 1970.

Hartley, Eugene L., and Hartley, Ruth. *Outside Readings in Psychology*. New York: Thomas Y. Crowell, 1957.

Hassinger, Jack, and Via, Murray. "How Much Does a Tutor Learn Through Teaching Reading." *Journal of Secondary Education* 44, no. 1 (January 1969): 42–44.

Hunter, Elizabeth. "A Cross-Age Tutoring Program Encourages the Study of Teaching in a College Methods Course." *Journal of Teacher Education* 19, no. 4 (Winter 1968): 447–451.

"Independent Projects by Teachers." Second annual summary of teacher reports, Sonoma County Schools, Santa Rosa, California, 1967.

Klucive, Mary Jean. "Self-Image and the First-Grade Pupil." *Ginn and Company Contributions in Reading* 23 (1964).

Lancaster, Joseph. *Improvements in Education*. London: Collins and Perkins, 1806.

Landrum, J. W., and Martin, M. D. "When Students Teach Others: One-to-One Project, Los Angeles Public Schools." *Education Leadership* 27, no. 5 (February 1970): 446–448.

LeBoeuf, Flores. "*Qui Docet Discit*—He Who Teaches, Learns." *The Science Teacher* 35, no. 1 (January 1968): 53–56.

Levine, Richard H. "Reaching Out for Danny." *American Education* 6, no. 6 (July 1970): 10–14.

Lippitt, Peggy. "Children Can Teach Other Children." *The Instructor* no. 9 (May 1969): 41 ff.

Lippitt, Peggy, Eiseman, Jeffrey, and Lippitt, Ronald. *Cross-Age Helping Program: Orientation, Training, and Related Materials*. Ann Arbor: University of Michigan, Center for Research on Utilization of Scientific Knowledge, Institute for Social Research, 1969.

Lippitt, Peggy, and Lohman, John E. "Cross-Age Relationships—An Educational Resource." *Children* 12, no. 3 (May–June 1965): 113–117.

Lutz, Jean M., and Stuart, Allaire. "Sixth-Grade Aides for the Kindergarten." *Aides to Teachers and Children*. Washington, D.C.: Association for Childhood Education International, 1968.

Mays, Billie. "Teen-Age Aides." *Aides to Teachers and Children*. Washington, D.C.: Association for Childhood Education International, 1968.

McCracken, Robert, Leaf, Bernice, and Johnson, Laura. "Individualizing Reading with Pupil Teachers." *Education* 86, no. 3 (November 1965): 174–176.

McCurdy, A., III. "Two-Way Street: A New Kind of Tutoring Program." *Independent School Bulletin* 29, no. 1 (October 1969): 25–27.

Melaragno, Ralph J., and Newmark, Gerald. "Tutorial Community Project: Report of the Second Year, July, 1969–August, 1970." Santa Monica, California: System Development Corporation, n.d.

National Commission on Resources for Youth. "Administrator's Memo." New York: NCRY, 1968.

———. "Final Report on Demonstration Project Proposal to Develop a Monitoring-Assessment System for Youth Tutoring Youth E&D Model In-School NYC Program." U.S. Department of Labor, Grant no. 42-9-12-134, June 30, 1969, to June 29, 1970.

———. "Final Report, In-School Neighborhood Youth Corps Project." Manpower Administration, Department of Labor, Contract no. 42-7-001-34, January 31, 1969.

———. "For The Tutor." New York: NCRY, 1970.

———. "A Manual for Trainers." New York: NCRY, 1970.

———. "Supervisor's Manual." New York: NCRY, 1968.

———. "Tutoring Tricks and Tips." New York: NCRY, 1970.

———. "A Tutor's Handbook." New York: NCRY, 1970.

———. "You're the Tutor:" New York: NCRY, 1968.

———. "Youth Tutoring Youth—It Worked." Report on an In-School Neighborhood Youth Corps Demonstration Project, Manpower Administration, Department of Labor, Contract no. 42-7-001-34, January 31, 1968.

Newmark, Gerald, and Melaragno, Ralph J. "Tutorial Community Project: Report on the First Year, May, 1968–June, 1969." Santa Monica, California: System Development Corporation, n.d.

Norton, Diana. "The 'Mutually Aided Learning' Project as Seen by the High School 'Learning Assistants,'" Cherry Creek Schools, Englewood, Colorado, n.d.

Page, William R. "Evaluation Report: The Tutoring Program." Brittany Junior High School, University City, Missouri, July 9, 1967.

Perkins, Charles. "A Leadership Techniques Course." *Journal of Health, Physical Education and Recreation* 37, no. 7 (September, 1966): 33–35.

Pinckney, Virgil. "The Teacher, Delinquent, and the Training School." *Michigan Education Journal* (January 1963): 356.

"Pint-Size Tutors Learn by Teaching." *American Education* (April 1967): 29.

Pollack, Cecelia, Sher, Norman, and Teitel, Beatrice. "Child Helps Child and Both Learn." Paper presented at the American Orthopsychiatric Association Annual Meeting, 1969.

"Project-CLINIC." San Miguel School, Sunnyside, California, n.d.

"Project Enable." Cooperative Project of the John F. Kennedy Center, George Peabody College for Teachers, Metropolitan Nashville School, Central Midwestern Regional Education Laboratory, Model Cities Agency, Nashville, Tennessee, n.d.

"A Proposed Study to Develop a Tutorial Community in the Elementary School." System Development Corporation, Santa Monica, California, 1968.

Riessman, Frank. "The 'Helper-Therapy' Principle." *Social Work* 10, no. 2 (April 1965): 27–32.

Riessman, Frank, and Alberts, Frank. "Digging 'The Man's' Language." *Saturday Review* (September 17, 1966): 80 ff.

Rime, Laura, and Ham, Jane. "Sixth-Grade Tutors." *The Instructor* 77, no. 7 (March 1968): 104–105.

Rosenshine, Barak, and Furst, Norma. "The Effects of Tutoring Upon Pupil Achievement: A Review of Research." Temple University, 1969.

Rosenthal, Robert, and Jacobson, Lenore. *Pygmalion in the Classroom: Teacher Expectation and Pupil's Intellectual Development.* New York: Holt, Rinehart and Winston, 1968.

Shapiro, Annette Frank, and Hopkins, Lee Bennett. "Pupil-Teachers." *The Reading Teacher* 21, no. 2 (November 1967): 128–129.

Silberman, Charles. "Murder in the Classroom, III." *Atlantic Monthly* (August 1970): 85–98.

Spencer, Darrell. "Neighborhood Youth Corps Tutorial Program." Raleigh, North Carolina, Public Schools, Summer 1970.

Stouffer, R. G., and Groff, P. "Should You Use Pupil Tutors?" *The Instructor* 77, no. 1 (August 1967): 35.

"Student Tutors for Floundering Classmates." *School Activities* 35, no. 8 (April 1964): 255–256.

Suchman, Edward. *Evaluative Research.* New York: Russell Sage Foundation, 1967.

"10-Year-Olds Are Tutoring 7-Year-Olds." *Education News* (January 22, 1968): 8.

Thelen, Herbert A. "The Humane Person Defined." Paper presented at the Secondary Education Leadership Conference, St. Louis, Missouri, November 1967.

———. "Learning by Teaching." Report of a Conference on the Helping Relationship in the Classroom," Stone-Brandel Center, University of Chicago, 1968.

————. "Tutoring by Students: What Makes It So Exciting?" *The School Review* 77, no. 3 (September 1969): 229–244.

Trasin, Walter. "Can Learners Teach?" *The Clearing House* 34, no. 5 (January 1960): 263–265.

Van Wessem, Katherine. "A Tutoring Program: The Second Year." Brittany Junior High School, University City, Missouri, July 9, 1967.

Weinstein, Gerald, and Fantini, Mario D. *Toward Humanistic Education, A Curriculum of Affect.* New York: Praeger Publications, 1970; published for the Ford Foundation.

Williams, Percy V. "School Dropouts." *NEA Journal* 52, no. 2 (February 1963): 8–10.

Wright, Benjamin. "Should Children Teach?" *Elementary School Journal* 60, no. 7 (April 1960): 353–369.

Wright, Elizabeth J. "Upper-Graders Learn by Teaching." *The Instructor* 78, no. 2 (October 1969): 102–103.

Yerry, Marie J. "Interage Classes in the Plainedge (New York) School District," n.d.

FILMS

The Helping Relationship. Thirty-minute color film based on a conference entitled "Learning by Teaching" at the University of Chicago, December 1968. W. Clement and Jessie Stone Foundation, Prudential Building, Chicago. Ill. 60601.

Youth Tutors Youth. Twenty-minute black-and-white film of YTY in Philadelphia and Washington, D.C., during the summer of 1968. National Commission on Resources for Youth, 36 West 44 Street, Room 1314, New York, N.Y. 10036.

INDEX

72 73 10 9 8 7 6 5 4 3 2